WHAT READERS ARE SAYING ABOUT

Extended: 150 Days of Inspiration for Students

"What a refreshing devotional for students to keep close at hand. God's Word never returns void. Expect breakthrough as you apply these Scriptures to your daily life."

—Dawna De Silva, Bethel Sozo

"The true gift of this devotional by Jasmine lies in the heart of the author—a loving heart completely full of profound trust and un-wavering faith in God. Noticing her sincere and gentle guidance, the readers will find insights into God's teaching that they can relate to, reflect on, and use to guide them in building their own personal relationship with Jesus Christ."

—Terri Beatty, Drama Instructor, Clare High School

"What can be said about a high school senior with the tenacity and discipline to lead her generation into being all that they can be for Jesus? Jasmine's devotional is the fruit of that discipline, packed full of godly wisdom and encouragement that reflects a heart of love for both God and her peers. I love the willingness of this lovely young lady to rise up and be a voice to her generation! Your student will be challenged to move beyond the status quo, produce real spiritual fruit, and encouraged to step into a living, abiding life with Jesus. What could be better than that?"

—Kimberly Waldie, author and lead pastor's wife, Living Hope Church in Traverse City, MI

"Jasmine's devotionals are full of great insight. She also brings great practical application by using personal examples from her own life. This is just the kind of writing that will engage students 'right where they live.'"

—Jeff Hlavin, Assemblies of God Michigan District Superintendent

"Jasmine Harper represents a generation of young women who are both talented and charismatic. What truly makes her stand out is an understanding of Scripture and commitment to teaching as demonstrated in *Extended: 150 Days of Inspiration for Students*."

—Josh Wellborn, Student Ministries Director, Michigan District Assemblies of God

"Not just a dynamic voice to her generation, but with depth, conviction, and clarity, Jasmine Harper's words are a challenge and an encouragement to all believers."

—Ron Kopicko, Spring Arbor University Chaplain

"An inspirational and daily reminder about the greater purpose of our lives and the gift that life truly is. Interwoven throughout each message are life's lessons and Jasmine's personal reflection of faith, which provide inspiration that we all can relate to."

—Kyle McKown, Clare High School Girls' Track & Field and Cross-Country Head Coach

"God knows people need others they can look to for encouragement and inspiration in following Christ. Using various Scripture, personal examples that include struggles and wins, and straight-to-the-heart points, Jasmine invites students of all ages to make their faith their own. Your student(s) will be encouraged to take a real look at their current life, grow in their relationship with Jesus *and* put it to good use!"

—Nick and Jill Nelson, Lead Pastors, Connect City Church, Battle Creek MI Assemblies of God Michigan District Fine Arts Festival Coordinators

"In the dictionary, you might find Jasmine Harper's picture next to the words 'Exceptional' and 'Humility.' In *Extended: 150 Days of Inspiration for Students*, she combines the simplicity of childlike faith with deep spiritual insight to both challenge and encourage students. At a time when most young ladies her age are concerned with how many followers they have on Instagram, it's wonderful to see Jasmine as an emerging leader share from her heart, her experiences, and God's Word."

—Rev. Rocky A. Barra, MA, BS, AA, Lead Pastor, Connection Church

"I enjoyed Jasmine's devotional. Such maturity and love for the Word of God. Just the beginning for this young lady and her faith walk!"

—Bonnie Rae Walter, Clare Fellowship of Christian Athletes (FCA) Huddle Leader of the oldest FCA Huddle in the state for nearly 30 years

"This book contains great wisdom, encouragement, and guidance that will help students who are young in their faith to start to understand how to grow in their relationship with Jesus. It has a very personal and refreshing feel from the author who is writing to her own generation and calling them to live a life full of Christ."

—Coach Bryan Burk, Spring Arbor University's Head Women's Track & Field and Cross Country Coach

"As I read this devotional for students I quickly realized that Jasmine has a deep relationship with Christ and wisdom beyond her years. It's clearly not just a devotional for students but for anyone who loves Jesus. Consider this your invitation to join Jasmine on her journey as she walks out her own faith."

—Mark Harper, pastor, filmmaker, and author of *The Red Book*, an Amazon #1 bestselling book

"This is outstanding reading! Jasmine is a very inspirational leader in our school and community. Her love of God and commitment to Jesus are true inspirations to all she comes in contact with. Jasmine's devotionals cover life and are written in a way to motivate the reader to turn to God when making various decisions. There is something for everyone in this book. I highly recommend this devotional! *Extended* is a must read for all ages."

—Coach Kelly Luplow, Head Football Coach (three decades plus), Clare High School, Michigan High School Football Hall of Fame

"Jasmine shares her heart by offering daily guidance and encouragement to young adults from a mature and grounded perspective. Her thoughts and stories of personal success and struggle speak hope and encouragement. *Extended: 150 Days of Inspiration for Students* leads readers into a daily discipline with a Bible selection and prayer for each day. The entries are deeply relatable and are written with conviction and clarity for a generation searching for answers."

—Joy Kleinhardt, business owner extraordinaire, Integrity Machine Services and Ground Level Packaging

"As she graduates from high school, there's much to admire about Jasmine Harper—track and cross country records and state championships, performing musically for audiences, completing high school with honors, and now her first book—but her greatest accomplishment is the life she lives for the Lord. This is evident as you read through this daily devotional. "For in him we live and move and have our being," Acts 17:28 (Day 24). You will be blessed and challenged as you read through this collection of inspirational readings!"

—Lori Van Veen, mother of two teenage daughters, follower of Jesus, volunteer children's / teen leader

"Jasmine Harper inspires readers to believe anything is possible with God. We recommend this 150-day journey to young people who aspire to hit the ground running to achieve their dreams in life."

—Mayra Troya-Nutt, MD, FACOG, Beaumont Health OB/GYN
—Jeffrey G. Nutt, JD; Fulbright Scholar, Oxford University 1986; Jeffrey G. Nutt & Associates, PLLC President; Fulbright Association Michigan Chapter President 2014-15; One University of the Americas Fund President; State Bar Champion of Justice 2007

"This is such a compelling, inspiring, and engaging devotional for students. It is relatable, simple, and full of words spoken from God. *Extended: 150 Days of Inspiration for Students* is something I recommend to all of my girls, and something I read to be filled, too. If you want to know God's heart, step deeper with the Spirit or be encouraged each day, start with this!"

—Reyna Luplow, Spring Arbor University alumnus, Director of *That Girl on Fire*

"Jasmine Harper shares timeless truths for all generations. The three-part format of her daily writings is clear and concise. They are based upon the truth of Scripture, her own personal application, and finally a heartfelt prayer . . . all in an effort to uplift and encourage. She points her readers to the ultimate source of life, love and happiness . . . Jesus Christ."

—Mark Anthony Nutt, MFA; Academic Coach, Wisconsin Indianhead Technical College; Education Specialist, Wisconsin

Department of Public Instruction; owner, Blue Rock Workshop LLC; President of the Board, Crossroads Outreach

"Deeply profound and engaging, Jasmine writes with wisdom and insight beyond her years. Her devotionals are helpful for any stage of life, but as parents of young children, we're excited to use these as discussion points for guiding their hearts and minds as they grow older."

—**Michael G. Swinger, MPT (Leelanau Physical Therapy) & Sarah Swinger ("Lord and Lady Swinger")**

"Jasmine displays the joy of the Lord. Her heart to encourage and stir up a deep faith in others is so evident through these devotionals. She is an example of what it means to live for Christ and glorify God in all things."

—**Jessica Hutchens, speaker, singer-songwriter, recording artist, Merit Award Winner for Worship Leading Solo at National Fine Arts, radio host, founder of Jessica Joy Ministries**

"I love the transparency and honesty found in these devotionals. Jasmine has covered a variety of topics that will be very relevant and helpful to students and beyond. Her insight was a blessing to me. I've known Jasmine her whole life and have had the pleasure of watching her grow into a beautiful woman of God. I know these devotionals have flowed from a heart that has spent much time with Jesus. She is an inspiration!"

—**Lisa Dewar, Teaching Leader and Weekly Lecturer / Greater Chicago Area Bible Study Fellowship**

"Jasmine is an amazing young woman and a beautiful writer. Her words are simple, yet I found them to be quite profound. While I know she was writing these daily prayers from the perspective of a student for other students, as an adult, I was compelled to open my heart and head to what she was sharing. I love the courage she expressed on Day 50—It made me think about whether or not I have courage enough in my own beliefs and love toward God. And, Day 40 is my favorite. It's not only one of my favorite Bible verses, it's also a stretch for life. I loved her simple prayer for that day."

—Patricia Ball, former Race Director of the Detroit Marathon, entrepreneur, Human Resource Director for the Buena Vista School District in Colorado

"Reading this devotional book makes our hearts leap with joy! Jasmine knows how to put into words that inner voice of a Christian facing different seasons, trials, and important decisions. How valuable this is for our young people! To have a voice rising up and speaking into their hearts the great spiritual truths, deep concepts of our faith, in a simple yet powerful 'sold out for Jesus' attitude. Jasmine Harper decided long ago to live out loud for Jesus. Jasmine, go as far as the Lord has planned, and as God told Jeremiah: 'Run with the horses.'" (Jeremiah 12:5)

—Pastor Adrian Falgetelli, Spring Arbor University graduate, family life educator

—Pastor Silvia L. Falgetelli, Futura Language Professionals Spanish Instructor, Hispanic Pastors at Emmanuel Christian Center, Spring Lake Park, MN

"This is the type of book I would have loved to have when I was a college student or my first couple of years out of college. It's so clear about what it means to walk out faith in Jesus and live the rewards."

—Maryanna Young, CEO Aloha Publishing

"The insights that Jasmine includes in these daily devotionals show the depth of her walk with Christ and her passion for young people to experience Jesus on a deeper level. Even as an adult, these devotionals spoke to my heart and challenged me. I can't wait to purchase this devotional for my daughter!"

—Jennifer Cook, Worship Team Administrative Assistant; Coordinator of New School Development and Contract Amendments, the Governor John Engler Center for Charter Schools, Central Michigan University

"Jasmine share's her loving relationship with God through her personal experiences and encourages others that they can have the same. Her words and simple prayers make it easy to understand how approachable God is to each of us."

—Donna Morris, mentor, youth leader, Grace Christian Church

"It's such a delight when you encounter a young woman whose love for God is so deep and pervasive that it literally permeates every waking moment of her life. Such is the case with Jasmine. Her love for God becomes obvious as you read her devotionals. Her insight and wisdom is not only contagious but filled with truths that will speak to anyone who has breath. Enjoy."

—Marlene Cummings, M.A., CCC-SLP, Speech/Language Pathologist, AAC Consultant

—Timothy Cummings, Summit-Global Leadership Alliance

EXTENDED

150

DAYS OF
INSPIRATION

for Students

JASMINE
HARPER

Extended: 150 Days of Inspiration for Students
By Jasmine Harper
Copyright © 2017 Jasmine Harper

Softcover ISBN: 978-0-9823356-1-1
eBook ISBN: 978-0-9823356-2-8
Library of Congress Control Number: 2017904060

Cover Design Direction: Lisa Harper and Jasmine Harper
Cover & Interior Design: Fusion Creative Works, fusioncw.com
Book Production: Aloha Publishing, Eagle, ID

Author Photos: Alloy Signature, AlloySignature.net

Published by VerticalView Publishing
PO Box 262, Clare, MI 48617
Phone: 734-775-3073
VerticalViewPublishing.com
MarathonMission.net

This book is available at ExtendedDevo.com.
Also available as softcover and ebook at online retailers, including Amazon.com.

Printed in the United States of America
First Edition 2017

"May our Lord Jesus Christ himself and God the Father, who loved us and by His grace gave us eternal encouragement and good hope, encourage your hearts and strengthen you in every good deed and word."

II Thessalonians 2:16-17

This book is dedicated to my parents for helping me achieve my goals. My mother keeps my life on track as a human planner. My dad never fails to make me laugh with crazy puns and is the loudest voice cheering for me at my track meets. Thank you both for showing me who Jesus is.

CONTENTS

Dear Friend,

I have so much joy in my heart in bringing you this devotional book. Writing has always been a hobby for me, but I did not start writing these messages with the intention of publishing them. I simply made a New Year's Resolution in 2015 that I would start writing daily devotionals. I never thought my devotional messages would bring me this far. In this book, you will find excerpts from myself—ages fourteen through eighteen. You will find stories of hardship and triumphs. Most importantly, you will find stories of the love of God, because I believe His love is present in both hardships and triumphs.

Whenever I am writing a song or a story, the title is one of the last things that comes to me. In the very early stages of this book, I would frequently get asked what I was calling it. I never had an answer until I had a special encounter with the Lord at the National Fine Arts Festival in 2016 in Louisville, Kentucky. Emmanuel LIVE was singing the song, "This Is Revival" (Open Up Our Eyes), and I heard the lyrics, "We stand with our arms extended. Our hearts, they belong to You."

In that moment, as I was worshiping with thousands of other teenagers, I knew there was something significant about that word, *extended*. To me, the simplicity of the title *Extended* has two meanings. We, as Christians, are His hands and feet extended. We should act out the goodness of the Lord every day for others to see. The second meaning describes how our relationship with Jesus should be a vertical relationship. We must lift our hands, faith, hopes, fears, dreams, love, and praise all to Jesus.

Use this devotional book any way you'd like—write in it and highlight it and make notes! You can read several excerpts in one day, or spread them out throughout the year. This is my prayer for this devotional book: that you will be encouraged, and that you will understand that the Creator of heaven is madly in love with you. I pray that this book will help you experience that love as you draw closer to Jesus. Thank you for taking this journey with me!

Blessings,

Jasmine

THE PERFECT BALANCE OF STRENGTH AND PEACE

**"The Lord gives strength to his people;
the Lord blesses his people with peace."**

— *Psalm* 29:11

This is one of my favorite verses in the Bible—and I hope it will become one of yours, too! God knows that strength and peace make the perfect balance. If someone has strength, but not peace, it will only carry him or her so far. Physical or emotional strength cannot and should not replace the calmness of one's heart. Having peace is learning to fully rely on God and trust Him. Peace is saying to yourself, "It is well with my soul." Peace is contentment. I believe amazing deeds for the sake of Christ start with peace (deciding in your heart that the Lord deserves our trust), and the peace is backed up by strength—God's strength! Ask yourself today how you can exemplify courage, confidence yet humility, and bravery.

PRAYER: Lord, I pray that in my life I would learn to have peace during tough situations. Let me have hope as I lean on Your strength, which makes me brave! I love You, Jesus. Amen.

notes:

NATURAL INSTINCTS

"Make sure that nobody pays back wrong for wrong, but always try to be kind to each other and to everyone else."

— *1 Thessalonians* 5:15

What is your natural instinct when you know people are talking about you? (Whether you're stuck in school or work drama, or you sailed that ship a long time ago, gossip isn't fun for anyone.) I would most likely be tempted to talk about how I don't like the "gossipers," or talk about their flaws. However, that is not what Jesus calls us to do. Luke 6:31 says, "Do unto others as you would have them do to you." A big part of being a Christian is having compassion and empathy for others, no matter how badly they treat you, and no matter how easy it is to gossip about them. Maybe you are labeled as the freaky Christian goody-two-shoes, like me! In moments when you are tested, have patience and ask for God's words to say.

PRAYER: Dear Jesus, I pray that You would give me wisdom as I face problems and people who do wrong to me. Thank You for showing me how to be kind to others through words and actions. Amen.

EVERYONE HAS SOMETHING

**"And whatever you do, whether in word or deed,
do it all in the name of the Lord Jesus,
giving thanks to God the Father through him."**

— *Colossians* 3:17

Isn't it amazing how God has called each of His children to have a uniquely fulfilled life? Everyone has something that he or she is good at. It could be singing, or maybe it's being handy with computers. Whatever it is, the Lord asks us to use our talents for Him. Make His name famous amidst the lost people who are trying desperately to make themselves famous. There are a million different ways to worship Jesus and seven billion people who deserve to know about Him. People will notice your areas of expertise, but what's most important is that they notice God through them.

PRAYER: Lord, thank You for the talents and gifts You have blessed me with. Help me to always remember that they come from You. I want to make Your name famous. Amen.

notes:

TRUSTING GOD

**"Do not let your hearts be troubled.
Trust in God, trust also in me."**

— *John 14:1*

Jesus was speaking this to His disciples when He told them that He was going up to Heaven. I'm sure it wasn't a very easy thing to understand. If Jesus said, "Hey, come follow me!" and then He "left" His followers on Earth, I would be pretty confused. But no one truly knew what Jesus had in store. He died to save us from our sins, and He rose from the dead. There was a time in my life when trusting God was the only thing I could do. I was injured for almost three months, partly during my cross-country season, and I was battling to recover the rest of the school year. It was really hard for me to understand, because I like to worship Jesus with my running. Yet, through it all, the Lord is faithful with abundant blessings to give. If you are struggling right now, trust in Jesus. I promise it's worth it!

PRAYER: Dear Jesus, sometimes I don't get why things happen in life. Remind me that You have a bigger plan in store. Help me to trust in You. Amen.

notes:

DON'T YOU KNOW?

"Do you not know? Have you not heard? The Lord is the everlasting God, the Creator of the ends of the earth. He will not grow tired or weary, and his understanding no one can fathom."

— *Isaiah 40:28*

We've all seen at least one movie with a cliché snobby teenager who shouts at his or her parents, "No one understands me!" (Probably seventy percent of those movies were made with Lindsay Lohan in the 2000s.) Truly, it's so awesome that the Creator of the Earth intentionally knows and understands everyone. Have you ever thought about the fact that even Jesus had bad days? He'll always be able to relate to you. He loves and cares for us so much, even though He doesn't have to. When relationships with people fail, God still stands firm. He'll never get tired of hearing your cries and desires. The comfort He has for you is everlasting.

PRAYER: God, thank You for understanding me even when I don't understand You. I will lean on You because Your strength and love are everlasting. Amen.

notes:

"Do not conform any longer to the pattern of this world, but be transformed by the renewing of your mind. Then you will be able to test and approve what God's will is— his good, pleasing and perfect will."

— *Romans 12:2*

You may have heard the saying, "Be in the world, not of it," (based on John 17:14). I think being in the world means compassionately recognizing daily and real problems. It means not putting on a mask or being too prideful to socialize with certain people. Yet, "of the world" means that you are just a piece that fits in the puzzle—part of the world's pattern in how it approaches life. The world is full of idols that people don't even realize they're worshiping. All good things come from God. All bad things and temptations are of this world. It's so important that what we watch, listen to, and think about are all wholesome things, allowing us to grow deeper in Him and see His will.

PRAYER: Father, please help me to resist the worthless temptations of this world while still reaching people of this world. Let me only think on good things. Amen.

"I think being in the world means compassionately recognizing daily and real problems. It means not putting on a mask or being too prideful to socialize with certain people."

DECLARE A PROMISE

" . . . God has said, 'Never will I leave you or forsake you.'
So we say with confidence, 'The Lord is my helper; I will
not be afraid. What can man do to me?'"

— Hebrews 13:5-6

Sadly, we will face days and meet people that bring disappointments. Society has lost the ability to be faithful and patient. Yet, God will never give up on you. It would simply be impossible! With the many promises God has made in His Word, why not declare a promise back to Him? Do it with confidence. Make your relationship personal. There is no reason to let fear enter your heart when you have the Lord as your Helper. He is always, always in control. Be like Captain America, ready to face what the world is throwing at you. God is your shield in times of trouble! So don't worry. What can man do to you?

PRAYER: Dear Jesus, thank You for being my Helper. I won't be afraid because I know You will never leave me. I love You. Amen.

DAY
8

BE THAT FRIEND

"A man that has friends must show himself friendly, and there is a friend that sticks closer than a brother."

— *Proverbs 18:24 (AKJV)*

There comes a time in life when people find out who their friends are. You could be in a situation with unloving friends. This verse doesn't say, "A friend loves when they get something good out of the relationship." No, it's describing a friend that goes out of his or her way to be like Jesus. Of course there are times when everyone messes up, but it's extremely important to surround yourself with people who honor the Word of God. What or whom you surround yourself with has a huge impact on you (garbage in; garbage out)! Be the friend that does something extra to make others feel special. Kindness never needs a reason.

PRAYER: Dear God, help me to be a loving friend who those around me can lean on. Please put godly people in my life who can help me grow in my relationship with You. Amen.

notes:

REMEMBERING HIM

**"Where, O death, is your victory?
Where, O death, is your sting?"**

— *1 Corinthians 15:55*

A couple of years ago, I realized that there are a lot of people who don't know the true meaning of Easter. We give a lot of attention to Christmas (which is good and fun). Yet, without Easter, all people would be drowning in their pool of sin with no life preserver in sight! Romans 6:23 says, "For the wages of sin is death, but the gift of God is eternal life in Christ Jesus." Every person ultimately deserves death, but Jesus made a way for us to be in Heaven with Him for eternity. He cares about us that much! Accepting the love of Jesus in your life saves you from the stress of death. Death has no mark or sting. Death is not victorious because Jesus won the victory.

PRAYER: Father, thank You for sending Your Son to die for me to pay my price. Teach me to remember what was done for me. I love You. Amen.

notes:

ABIDE AND REMAIN

"Remain in me, and I will remain in you. No branch can bear fruit by itself; it must remain in the vine. Neither can you bear fruit unless you remain in me."

— *John* 15:4

As followers of Christ, everything in our lives should connect back to Jesus. This is just how fruit is connected to the Vine. The fact is, we need Jesus desperately. There is no life without Him. If you want God's favor, it's important to honor Him. Intentionally seeking out a personal relationship with Him is how to remain in Jesus. If one person in a marriage purposefully talks to his or her spouse only once a week, how would they be considered close? Since we are the Bride of Christ, talking to God should be even more important to us. Keep your foundation firm in the Lord!

PRAYER: Jesus, I want to remain in You always. Help me to stay close to You and follow Your ways. Amen.

notes:

"The fact is that we need Jesus desperately. There is no life without Him."

CAN YOU BELIEVE IT?

"For I am going to do something in your days that you would not believe."

— *Habakkuk* 1:5

God has so much in store for His children. Sometimes it can take a while to figure out what the Lord is doing. But, maybe it's a good thing that we don't always know. If we knew everything, we would be on the same pedestal as Jesus, which is not how it is meant to be! And, we would probably go into hiding, avoiding the time of spiritual strength training. God often takes us on a detour before we reach our destination, experiencing a different part of life we would have otherwise overlooked. As a young middle school student, I never would have believed that I would get the cross-country record for my high school as a freshman. I was so thankful to God. The Lord has blessings for everyone—blessings you couldn't even believe! Be excited for what He has planned.

PRAYER: Dear Lord, thank You for having great things in store for me. Let me remember all of the blessings You've given me. Amen.

notes:

DAY 12

LET YOUR WORDS HAVE MEANING

"Do not let any unwholesome talk come out of your mouths, but only what is helpful for building others up according to their needs, that it may benefit those who listen."

— *Ephesians 4:29*

Many times people can become so numb to vulgarity that it barely fazes them anymore. Their conscience is seared. As Christians, it's critical to know that what we say should represent Jesus. Let's face it . . . People (especially teenagers) are pretty nosey. They will remember things you say and see what you post on social media. Words are so powerful, so let yours have meaning! What do you want to be remembered for? Would you feel ashamed if parents, teachers, and co-workers quoted your everyday language? What comes out of your mouth is a reflection of your heart. Choose today to speak words that would please Jesus.

PRAYER: God, I am sorry that my words are not always pleasing to You. I want my words to build others up for Your sake. Amen.

notes:

THE WILD RIDE OF ANXIETY

"Cast all your anxiety on him because he cares for you."

— 1 Peter 4:7

Anxiety is defined as "a feeling of worry, nervousness, or unease, typically about an imminent event or something with an uncertain outcome." I'd say that definition is pretty accurate. Even though I'm still a young adult, I've had my fair share of stressed-out moments . . . Like getting sick minutes before receiving All-State honors in track. Growing up, I also had to make a lot of school changes. I went from homeschooling to a Christian school to two separate public schools in a matter of five years. Putting myself out there and meeting new people was not easy. God wants you to throw away your worry. Life becomes a whole lot brighter when you realize that Jesus cares enough to take away all your burdens. The next time you're anxious, think about all God has brought you through. Let past experiences give you determination to conquer whatever comes your way.

PRAYER: Lord, I want to let go of all my anxieties. Help me to remember that You are always near, even in the hardest moments. Amen.

INTENTIONAL ACTS OF LOVE

"Dear children, let us love not with words or tongue, but with action and truth."

— 1 John 3:18

What is love? If you're scrolling down your newsfeed on Instagram, you'd probably see food that someone just loves, as well as their new favorite outfit that they love. Apparently a Man Crush Monday is the ultimate testament of love! My point is this: The word "love" is thrown around quite a bit. I'm guilty of it as much as anyone else. While showing love to friends is great, intentionally acting out love to others is meaningful, too. That doesn't mean liking or pinning a picture of a Bible verse and calling it good. One way to demonstrate real love is having empathy for people during situations that aren't your problems and offering help. Another example of love can occur when others get hot-tempered—sometimes our demonstration of love can be to not say anything at all. Here's a challenge: see how many people you can truly love today.

PRAYER: Dear Jesus, help me to act out in love to those around me. Teach me what love really means. Amen.

DAY
15

HOW SMART IS GOD?

"But the wisdom that comes from heaven is first of all pure; then peace-loving, considerate, submissive, full of mercy and good fruit, impartial and sincere."

— *James* 3:17

Have you ever stopped to think about just how smart God is? In fact, "smart" doesn't even do Him justice, because that word is held by worldly standards. He knows everything—and He's right by your side! Jesus wants us to ask Him what decisions to make and how to live our lives. What He says will never lead you astray. The Lord is incapable of manipulating. The verse above also shares specifically that His wisdom is considerate and full of mercy. God knows our hearts and desires. If you need help, all you really have to do is ask Him. Jesus is present, and His wisdom is real.

PRAYER: Father, there are many moments in my life when I simply don't know what to say or do. Help me to remember to call upon Your name for Your wisdom. Amen.

notes:

"You are the salt of the earth. But if the salt loses its saltiness, how can it be made salty again? It is no longer good for anything, except to be thrown out and trampled by men. You are the light of the world. A city on a hill cannot be hidden."

— *Matthew* 5:13–14

When I was younger, I honestly had no idea how this salt analogy made sense. All salt really does is just sit in a shaker, right? What this verse is explaining is that salt gives flavor to food just as Christians are to give flavor—and more—to the world. If you ate a pretzel without salt, something would taste rather empty, right? The *Fire Bible: Student Edition* shares, "Salt has healing properties, just as Christ's followers must bring healing to people who are hurting physically, emotionally, and spiritually." In addition, we are supposed to bring light and love to a world that is filled with darkness and hate. Be the salt.

PRAYER: Lord, help me to stand out for You in this world. I want to shine Your light to lead others to You. Amen.

notes:

"We are supposed to bring light and love to a world that is filled with darkness and hate.

Be the salt."

HOW CAN YOU GIVE?

"It is more blessed to give than receive."

— *Acts* 20:35

We were put on the Earth to love God and love people. Though people should choose to love themselves, loving yourself isn't the most important thing. Think about how much you could accomplish for others in the time you spend thinking about yourself. Jesus' followers in the Bible barely thought about themselves at all. As soon as Paul got out of prison for speaking about Jesus, he looked for even more ways to give and share the Word of God. "Giving" can come in many different forms. I believe it's intentionally sharing with others in a way that God has blessed you. It could be something you're good at, or maybe something you need a lot of. It could be your time. We can try as hard as we want to give from our own hearts, but ultimately it is only God's power that can make us capable to give and experience His miracles. No matter what you do, I encourage you to strive for greater things than just what you want.

PRAYER: Dear Jesus, thank You for what You've blessed me with. Please humble me so I can give it to others who are in need. Amen.

PLEASING MEN OR PLEASING GOD

"Am I now trying to win the approval of men, or of God? Or am I trying to please men? If I were still trying to please men, I would not be a servant of Christ."

— *Galatians* 1:10

Everyone is looking for some sort of satisfaction. Though Christians should love others continually, it is not the Christian's job to please others—it's to please Christ. There were certainly a lot of people who weren't pleased by Jesus. We shouldn't expect everyone to respond to the gospel with open arms, but that doesn't require the need to stop spreading His truth altogether! If someone is truly after God's own heart, what others think of him or her becomes completely irrelevant. Don't fall into the trap of wanting the acceptance of the world when the acceptance of Jesus is right in front of you! Run toward Him and pick up as many people as you can along the way.

PRAYER: God, I never want to be embarrassed about my faith. Help me to not worry about what others think, because You are who is most important. Amen.

notes:

HIS PLANS ARE UNSTOPPABLE

"Then Job answered the Lord, 'I know that you can do everything and that your plans are unstoppable.'"

— *Job 42:1–2*

You might be thinking, "Sure, it's easy to say that God can do everything if you have the picture-perfect life." Actually, Job had the furthest thing from a perfect life. He lost all his family members and everything he owned—and his friends were convinced it was because Job had committed some great sin. They were wrong—God was testing him. Maybe you're experiencing a Job time right now. Just know that after all of the trials, God proved Himself faithful to Job. The Lord wants to prove Himself faithful in your life, too. God's plans may not be our definition of good, but He could be using them to inspire others, just like Job's faithfulness despite his circumstances can be used to inspire you!

PRAYER: Dear Lord, when I am going through rough times, remind me of what Job was able to overcome through You. You are the same today that You were then. Amen.

notes:

EXPAND YOUR HORIZON

"Do nothing out of selfish ambition or vain conceit, but in humility consider others better than yourselves."

— *Philippians* 2:3

I think the young adult generation really needs to focus on this verse (including me). It seems as if people are either lifting themselves up or openly tearing themselves down. And, a lot of people tear others down to lift themselves up. Paul isn't explaining here that people should think, "I wish I could be like everyone around me. I'm not special." No! Not at all. Jesus has given each person special qualities. Paul is explaining to put the needs of others before your own. Expand your horizon and go out of your way to build someone else up. Being a Christian means depending on God because we don't have it all together. That's where humility steps in—to help Christians relate to others or see people as Christ sees them. We must acknowledge that God has the master plan.

PRAYER: Jesus, please help me to always stay humble and love who You created me to be at the same time. Let me think about others more than I think about myself. Amen.

"Expand your horizon and go out of your way to build someone else up."

DAY
21

SET AN EXAMPLE

"Don't let anyone look down on you because you are young, but set an example for the believers in speech, in life, in love, in faith and in purity."

— 1 Timothy 4:12

Jesus views every person the same way. Of course there are special things everyone has that Jesus loves, but He certainly doesn't target a certain age group to fulfill His duties. Samuel was a young boy who was just getting to know God when God spoke to him prophetically. Daniel was a teenager when the Lord put it on his heart to go against the crowd and stand up for what was right. No matter what age you are— still in your single digits, or nearing the triple digits—Jesus has things in store for you right now that are personal. The verse above says that the younger generation should be an example to believers. Be open to those who are young. They can think about things in a new way, and can teach us all a lesson about faith.

PRAYER: Father, never let me use my age as an excuse for not stepping out in faith. Help me to also be open to what those who are younger than me have to say. In Your name, Amen.

DAY
22

ONE OF THOSE DAYS

"So do not throw away your confidence; it will be richly rewarded. You need to persevere so that when you have done the will of God, you will receive what he has promised."

— *Hebrews* 10:36

Are you having one of "those" days? Maybe you're running late to school and your swimsuit falls out of your bag in the hallway. No one who sees bothers to tell you. Instead, your teacher picks it up and shows it to her class—asking whose it is, and you feel completely embarrassed. Okay, that's not completely relatable to a lot of people, but it did happen to me in eighth grade! In those moments, or even in bigger moments in life, it's crucial to remember that our hope and joy should not rely on what happens around us. We have a much firmer foundation that our confidence can and should depend on— Jesus! Your swimsuit won't be in the school hallway forever. Days pass and embarrassment turns into funny stories to tell, all because of something called perseverance.

PRAYER: Dear God, when I am having bad days, or weeks, or even years, I want to have my confidence on Your firm foundation. What You have promised is so much greater than what life throws at me. Amen.

"Forget the former things; do not dwell on the past. See, I am doing a new thing! Now it springs up, do you not perceive it?"

— Isaiah 43:18–19

It can be really easy to stay stuck in the past. We have good experiences that we wish would have lasted forever—such as a time when you felt a "spiritual high." Afterwards, the comparisons come . . . "If only my life were like that again. Jesus was moving so much more then." Wrong! Jesus is the same yesterday, today, and tomorrow. Another way to be stuck in the past is through negative memories. Somehow we strike up the nerve to declare that what has been done to us is bigger than God. Instead of moving forward in His direction, we just sit, going nowhere. God has new plans full of hope for every season. Trust in Him!

PRAYER: Dear Lord, I never want to limit Your power to overcome the past. Remind me that You make all things new, and You give me new beginnings. Amen.

notes:

CAN THEY TELL?

"For in him we live and move and have our being . . ."

— *Acts 17:28*

There is no true life without Jesus. The reason you and I are even alive is to bring glory to God and lead others to Him. That's why not a single day of our lives should be wasted. If Jesus died to give us something as special and great as life, how could we ignore it? All of our morals should point directly to Christ. Can people tell that you are a Christian just by who you are? Or would they have to look a little deeper? Following Jesus isn't reserved for one day of the week—it's a continual relationship! What you do is a representation of Christ. Make sure you're living up to it and making every moment a moment to serve Him!

PRAYER: Dear Jesus, thank You so much for the gift of life You gave me. Show me what to do so I can reflect who You are. I pray that the center of who I am would be rooted in You. I love You. Amen.

notes:

DAY 25

MAKE IT COUNT

"For the Lamb at the center of the throne will be their shepherd; he will lead them to springs of living water. And God will wipe away every tear from their eyes."

— *Revelation 7:17*

For most people, the topic of what goes on after their death is pretty uncomfortable. I mean, if you don't have your hope in God, that would be pretty unsettling, right? Heaven is such a beautiful place . . . It can't go unseen. Why not invite those around you to check it out? This verse says that God will be on the throne in Heaven, leading His people. One second physically in front of God is better than an entire lifetime on Earth. Notice the kind of water in Heaven—living water! It would be impossible to find a trace of death in Heaven, or even a tear. God will relieve everyone from his or her sadness. No one knows the day Jesus will return to take those who love and serve Him to Heaven. In the meantime, make your life count!

PRAYER: Dear God, thank You for giving me eternal life. I can't wait to be in Heaven with You. Let me live my life to its full potential before I get there. Amen.

"Perhaps this is the moment for which you have been created."

— *Esther* 4:14

God knows everything that will happen in our lives. Even before Rosa Parks was born, He knew that she would stay seated in that bus seat. She was created to change the world. You are, too! The time I felt this verse the strongest was the day my grandma died. My sister, Victoria, and I sang worship songs and hymns to her on her deathbed. She was actually singing along with us the day before. I felt extremely honored to bring comfort to my grieving family members through singing praises to Jesus and my grandma, as she breathed her last breaths. This verse, Esther 4:14, comes to mind when I think of my sister and me on that day; it has become a personal confirmation from God that I should use my singing for His glory. Maybe you've had a moment when God works through you so clearly. Never doubt His ability to create divine appointments in each day.

PRAYER: Father, thank You for creating me to do special things; I always want to seek Your presence. Amen.

"Maybe you've had a moment when God works through you so clearly. Never doubt His ability to create divine appointments in each day."

> **"He said to them, 'Go into all the world and preach the good news to all creation.'"**
>
> — *Mark* 16:15

These last words that Jesus spoke before He went to Heaven are known as The Great Commission. Usually someone's last words are pretty important! Jesus could have chosen anything to say, but this is what He wanted to leave His followers with. Now, "All the world" can mean whatever you make of it. Where you are presently is a part of the world, right? Sometimes I have this view of traveling really far and expecting to do extravagant things for Christ (which isn't bad at all!), but I think we can easily forget that we are in a mission field right now. Your friends and family around you who think they've got it all together need Jesus, too! If the love of God is meant to change our lives, why should we be scared to talk about it?

PRAYER: Dear Jesus, I want to answer Your call and follow Your last words. Give me opportunities and strength to share who You are, and open my eyes to see them. I love You. Amen.

notes:

DAY 28

BE PREPARED

" . . .We are looking forward to a new heaven and a new earth, the home of righteousness. So then, dear friends, since you are looking forward to this, make every effort to be spotless, blameless and at peace with him."

— 2 Peter 3:13–14

In school, did you ever have an assignment where the teacher didn't set a specific due date? In those situations, it shows the difference between those who like to prepare and those who like to procrastinate! I don't know about you, but I want to be prepared for the test when Jesus comes! People can spend so much of their lives putting off the subject of Heaven. This is the reality: Jesus is coming back. Since it hasn't happened yet, it's more and more likely every day. Of course, no one can predict the day that the world will end (not even the Mayans, who predicted the end of the world would occur in 2012), so that's why it's important to not waste a single moment of sharing the love of Jesus.

PRAYER: Dear Lord, thank You that Your Son is coming back! Help me to be motivated and passionate about being a Christ follower until then. Amen.

DAY 29

FREEDOM IS A GIFT

"You, my brothers, were called to be free. But do not use your freedom to indulge the sinful nature; rather, serve one another in love."

— *Galatians* 5:13

There are many who wonder why God allows people to do bad things. Part of the answer is free will. If everyone were robots programmed to do all the same things and respond exactly as other robots, they wouldn't be able to truly experience the love of God. They wouldn't be able to make the decision for themselves—to follow the Lord or not. Aren't you glad you're not a robot? Freedom is a gift that is often overlooked. This verse is a reminder to not take advantage of it. Use God's blessings to make wise choices and to advance His kingdom! Some people use freedom to become rebellious. I say we use it to compel us.

PRAYER: God, I never want to take advantage of the freedom You have given me. Please give me wisdom and strength to love others instead of sin. Amen.

notes:

DAY
30

WHAT'S THE SECRET?

"But godliness with contentment is great gain."

— 1 Timothy 6:6

Do you ever wonder why the people with the most "stuff" often have the worst attitudes? They try to fill their lives with the many things they can buy with money. Or there's the teenage girl that just *has* to have a boyfriend. She's not happy otherwise. Philippians 4:13, written by Paul, has to be one of the most well-known verses in the Bible: "I can do all things through Christ who gives me strength." Yet, a lot of people don't realize what comes before it. Philippians 4:12 says, "I know what it is to be in need, and I know what it is to have plenty. I have learned the secret of being content in any and every situation . . ." So the secret of being content is relying on God's strength during your day-to-day life. While the material world may seem glamorous, only God can give you a truly fulfilling and satisfying life.

PRAYER: Dear God, thank You so much for the blessings You've given me. Help me to be content no matter what my situation is. Remind me of what Paul went through, and remind me of the secret of contentment. Amen.

"So the secret of being content is relying on God's strength during your day-to-day life. Only God can give you a truly fulfilling and satisfying life."

DAY
31

LIVING WITH POWER

"Still others, like seed sown among thorns, hear the word; but the worries of this life, the deceitfulness of wealth and the desires for other things come in and choke the word, making it unfruitful."

— *Mark 4:18–19*

God's Word, the Bible, is living with power! Sometimes we can be worried about the wrong things; what God is trying to say goes in one ear and out the other. Perhaps you are focusing all your time on getting more money when Jesus is trying to teach you to give it away. The word "choke" doesn't exactly bring to mind sunshine and rainbows. Do you want the things in your life to choke Scriptures, or lead people to Scripture? These verses in Mark go on to say that some people accept the Word "and produce a crop—thirty, sixty, or even a hundred times what was sown." Strive to invest in the lives of others through the power of Jesus and His Word.

PRAYER: Dear Jesus, I don't want to replace You with unimportant things in my life. Let me dig deep in the Bible, and share the truths of Scripture with those around me. I love You. Amen.

DAY 32

FAMILY CHOICES

"But as for me and my household, we will serve the Lord."

— *Joshua 24:15*

No one really gets to choose the family they're born into. Maybe you have a close relationship with your family, or maybe it's just the opposite. When families come together to decide that their foundation is in the Lord, it is really significant. Children grow up looking at the examples of their parents. If you grew up in a tough situation, far from God, make a commitment that your future household will serve Him. The people who are around you daily affect you more than anyone, but you also have the opportunity to influence them. God has given you your family for a reason. Shine the light of the Lord brightly toward them, offering mercy and love.

PRAYER: Father, help my family to make it a priority to follow You. I want to be a good example of a Christian to the close people around me. Thank You for giving me my family. Amen.

notes:

YOUR TREASURE—YOUR HEART

"For where your treasure is, there will your heart be also."

— *Matthew 6:21*

This verse is basically saying your motives show what is most important to you. There are a lot of people who try to fake the outward appearance of their "treasure." But, God sees everyone for who he or she really is. Philippians 4:8 reads, "Whatever is true, whatever is noble, whatever is right, whatever is pure, whatever is lovely, whatever is admirable—if anything is excellent or praiseworthy—think about such things." Make sure that what is most important to you matches up with God's best for your life. Each and every day, we are all surrounded by examples of worldly treasures. The pressure of what the world wants is not going to lessen. How determined are you to find the Lord's treasure? I can assure you that it will be better than anything the world advertises.

PRAYER: God, I pray that the things that are most important to me are godly. Forgive me for putting my desires in front of Your treasure for me. Amen.

notes:

**"Yet I hold this against you:
You have forsaken your first love."**

— *Revelation 2:4*

Relationships are very sacred and special. Wedding vows aren't said for nothing, right? Just as a man and woman are to stay faithful, we (the Bride of Christ) must remain faithful to Jesus. Some may have the impression that God changes once all of the hype and excitement leaves. Wrong. If you think God is the One who has changed, reflect on yourself. Have you forgotten your first love? Check to see if a heart for Christ is really what you're after. You can't have a one-way relationship with Jesus. He'll always still love you no matter what, but being a follower of Him means doing your part, too. "Your part" includes connecting God to all aspects of your life and spending personal time with Him. Think of all that Jesus has done for you! Don't forsake your first love.

PRAYER: Dear Jesus, let me always strive to know You better. Please prevent me from downplaying who You are. I want to try harder to be more like You. Amen.

DAY
35

LET'S DO SOMETHING

" . . . The hour has come for you to wake up from your slumber, because our salvation is nearer now than when we first believed."

— *Romans 13:11*

Live like you're dying. Live every day as if it could potentially be your last day—not thinking about second chances. If it was said two thousand years ago that Jesus was coming back soon, think about how much time we have presently! The Rapture certainly isn't something to be scared of, but it is a reality. If Jesus came back today, would you say that you lived a fulfilled life? Wake up from sleeping and be active in your faith as a Christian! No one likes a teammate who doesn't try or just stands and watches. Stop waiting around and do something, both figuratively and literally. Often times, when I tell myself I'm going to take a twenty-minute nap, it turns into an hour nap, or longer! Don't let a quick power nap in your Christian faith turn into a sleep longer than what was intended. Stay tuned to what the Lord is saying. Jesus is coming, y'all!

PRAYER: Lord, help me remember that You are coming back to Earth. I want to do all I can for Your glory before that day comes. Amen.

DAY
36

FEARFULLY AND WONDERFULLY MADE

"For you created my inmost being; you knit me together in my mother's womb. I praise you because I am fearfully and wonderfully made."

— Psalm 139:13-14

The Bible clearly states that life is sacred and important—whether the person is born or unborn. That includes your life. Many times people think they need to be in a relationship to be happy. But, you need to be fully content with yourself before you try to make your life work with someone else. God created you in His image, and you're wonderful just by being you! The minute you start comparing yourself to others, it becomes a dark trap, which is hard to get out of. The girl you think is so much prettier than you may wish she could look like someone else. The guy you think is so much stronger than you probably still wants to be stronger than the next guy. It's honestly one massive circle of sad self-doubt. The Lord knew who you were even before you breathed your first breath. He created you, and He doesn't make mistakes.

PRAYER: God, teach me to be confident in the person You created me to be. I want to share the message that everyone is beautiful because they were made in Your image. Amen.

"The Lord knew who you were even before you breathed your first breath. He created you, and He doesn't make mistakes."

DAY
37

"For you know the grace of our Lord Jesus Christ, that though he was rich, yet for your sakes he became poor, so that you through his poverty might become rich."

— 2 Corinthians 8:9

Often, it's very easy for me to forget what Jesus has done. You may have heard it a thousand times that Jesus rose from the grave, but don't become so numb to it that the story loses all meaning in your heart. Jesus is perfect. He gave up everything to give us everything. In the verse above, it isn't specifically talking about money. God could be calling you to give up some of your "riches" or time so that others may be rich in Him. Eternal life with Jesus Christ is the biggest blessing one could receive. Don't take that opportunity for granted. Jesus didn't have to come to Earth as a human and die. But He saw something the world needed and gave it. We should do the same.

PRAYER: Dear Jesus, thank You for paying the ultimate sacrifice for me. Give me the courage to sacrifice for others for Your glory. Amen.

notes:

THE LOUDEST VOICE

**"My sheep listen to my voice;
I know them, and they follow me."**

— John 10:27

When I am running a cross-country or track race, there is always one voice I can hear above the others . . . my dad's. Not only is he the loudest one giving advice on how to race, but a lot of the words he says are very personal. It shows that we have developed a relationship. My dad is extremely smart with running (being that he was an All-American track athlete in college), so I know I can always trust his judgment. This is a representation of how God calls for us. He might be shouting, "Run faster from what's behind/tempting you." The Lord is the wisest One you'll ever meet. He knows what will happen in the future. The Bible also says that we can ask for wisdom, like Solomon, and He will give it to us as we listen to His voice. Sheep wouldn't follow a shepherd if they didn't trust him. Place your trust and hope in God. Take the time to get to know Him, because He knows even the deepest parts of you.

PRAYER: Lord, show me how to follow Your ways and listen to Your voice. My trust is in You. I love You, God! Amen.

TWO PEOPLE ARE BETTER THAN ONE

"Two people are better than one because together they have a good reward for their hard work. If one falls, the other can help his friend get up."

— Ecclesiastes 4:9–10a

You don't have to walk through life all alone! In God's Word, "iron sharpens iron" is used as a metaphor for how Christians should build each other up. By building someone else up, you're also having a positive effect on yourself. When I think of someone that always encourages me in my faith, I think of my friend, Lauryn. Even in middle school, she would give me devotionals to read and study. She is never afraid to hold me accountable in my faith. If you don't have friends in your life that you can count on to keep you accountable, just ask for some! What you talk/think about is a reflection of your heart. Positive talk makes a positive heart. Just as one might want supportive people around him or her to be encouragers in daily life, be that support system for someone else. Church isn't meant to be treated as a revolving door with people going in just to go out. Make an effort to spend time with the people in your life.

PRAYER: Dear God, please surround me with people who glorify You and people who teach me to do the same. Amen.

DAY
40

MAKE ACTS OF KINDNESS A HABIT

"The entire law is summed up in a single command: 'Love your neighbor as yourself.'"

— *Galatians* 5:8

One time someone told me a story of when they were at McDonald's paying for their food. They didn't have enough change, so they left to find some. When they came back, the person behind them had paid for their meal! That is showing love. If Jesus could turn the smallest bit of fish and bread into enough to feed 5,000, imagine how many McDonald's meals He could make out of a single Happy Meal! He would probably be crowned the new Ronald McDonald (McJesus?). Okay, maybe I am fantasizing a little, but it is true that we don't have to make random acts of kindness unfamiliar to us. Think about what you do for yourself every single day. Jesus calls us to spend an equal amount of time, or maybe even more, showing others that He cares!

PRAYER: Father, I want to follow in Your footsteps. Guide me in my daily life to try and love my neighbor like I love myself. Thank You for loving me. Amen.

"It is true that we don't have to make random acts of kindness unfamiliar to us."

DAY
41

LOVE AND HONOR

"Honor your father and your mother, so that you may live long in the land the Lord your God is giving you."

— *Exodus 20:12*

Sometimes it seems like a parent is one of the biggest blessings that is taken for granted. It breaks my heart when I hear people say thoughtless things—like they hate talking to their mom or they hate giving their dad hugs. Even though parents make mistakes too, keep in mind that it saves a lot of trouble to respect them. Are you the type of son or daughter you would want for a kid? If the answer is "no," then change your ways! The verse above is one of the Ten Commandments. What is important to God should be important to us also. By loving your parents, you're not just honoring them, but you're honoring the Lord. Shoot your parents a text right now, or give them a call, to tell them you're thankful for them and appreciate all they do for you!

PRAYER: Dear Jesus, give me patience and understanding in my relationship with my parents. I pray that You would mold me into a good example for my future children. Amen.

notes:

MAKE IT YOUR HEART'S CRY

"The Lord then said to Noah, 'Go into the ark, you and your whole family, because I have found you righteous in this generation.'"

— *Genesis 7:1*

I'm sure when Noah realized that God's plan for his life was to build a huge boat, he was slightly confused. Sometimes it's really hard to figure out the meaning behind our challenging times. Noah probably didn't think that his obedient act would be a historical tale told for thousands of years! This verse shows that God thought of Noah as righteous. When you go through times that are hard to understand, remember how God chose Noah (who was very faithful) to complete an important task. You never know what the Lord has in store for you. Genesis 7:5 says, "Noah did all that the Lord commanded him." Make it your heart's cry to be obedient to God.

PRAYER: God, help me to remember that there is a reason for everything. Even when I don't understand, You work all things out for good, just like You did for Noah. I love You, Lord. Amen.

notes:

WILL YOU ACCEPT THE PRIZE?

"Brothers, I do not consider myself yet to have taken hold of it. But one thing I do: Forgetting what is behind and straining toward the goal to win the prize for which God has called me heavenward in Christ Jesus."

— *Philippians 3:13–14*

These verses basically describe the purpose of living a life to honor God. Think about how incentives make such a big difference in competitions or just life in general. If a teacher offers kids candy for answering a question, their hands will constantly be raised. God has offered us a prize much greater than plastic-wrapped candy! Paul knows that life before Heaven isn't easy. He acknowledges in verse 13 that he doesn't have it all together, either. When you become a Christian, you are transformed and made new. Don't focus on the negativity of your past, instead focus on the hope of the future! Will you accept the prize?

PRAYER: Dear Lord, help me to always strive for what You have in me. I always want to keep my hope in You. Amen.

notes:

DAY 44

HOT OR COLD

"I know your deeds, that you are neither cold nor hot. I wish you were either one or the other! So, because you are lukewarm—neither hot nor cold— I am about to spit you out of my mouth."

— *Revelation* 3:15–16

If you have been in church for a while, you've probably heard many sermons preached on this subject of comparing people to temperatures. Yet, don't let it lose its meaning. These verses explain that being "hot" is like being on fire for God or really passionate about Him. Being "cold" is just the opposite—running away from a relationship with Jesus. God sees our hearts and what's truly inside. We can fake things all we want for the people around us, but He won't be fooled. I don't know about you, but I don't want to be the type of water that God spits out! Don't be on the fence. Choose one side or the other, because whether you realize it or not, being lukewarm is not something God accepts. I hope you choose to follow Jesus, because there's literally no better or more fulfilling decision in the world.

PRAYER: Dear Jesus, I want to be totally "on fire" for You. Help me to live out my faith every day and keep me from becoming lukewarm. Amen.

DAY 45

PATIENCE IN THE PLAN

**"The end of a matter is better than its beginning,
and patience is better than pride."**

— *Ecclesiastes 7:8*

My sophomore year of high school definitely tested my patience. That previous summer, I had several foot injuries. What was supposed to heal in six weeks ended up healing in three months. It was not always easy to watch my cross-country season go by after I had broken school records my freshman year. It felt like I needed to have an endless supply of patience. Every day was unpredictable. Ecclesiastes 7:8 explains that patience should be ranked higher than pride. It's okay to admit that you can't "do life" on your own. We all desperately need God's help. When the doctor wrapped my foot and put it in a boot for the second time, I remember hopelessly crying out to Jesus in confusion. I didn't understand. Yet, I had to hold on to the hope that God's plan was better than what I could see. You're capable of holding onto that same hope. Have patience in God's plan for your life.

PRAYER: Father, there are many times when it's hard to be patient and wait for all the answers. Let me trust in You and Your master plan. Amen.

PERSEVERANCE IN THE RACE

"Therefore, since we are surrounded by such a great cloud of witnesses, let us throw off everything that hinders and the sin that so easily entangles. And let us run with perseverance the race marked out for us."

— Hebrews 12:1

It's so cool to me that Jesus literally has billions and billions of people's lives planned out. He is like our coach in this race of life! Some people just don't realize the value of being on His team. Not only are we supposed to have faith in our "coach," but also perseverance. If an athlete who runs the two mile in track doesn't have perseverance, he or she not only won't win the race, but may not even finish the race. So, do everything on your part to make this race easy for yourself. Throw away the burdens of self-doubt or insecurity. Pitch the bad memories that are as heavy as your backpack during the week of finals! Lastly, remember that God is always running this race with you.

PRAYER: Dear God, please show me how to get rid of what is not pleasing to You. Thank You for planning out my life and caring about me. Amen.

"Christ is like our coach in this race of life! Some people just don't realize the value of being on His team."

THE POWER OF PRAYER

"Devote yourselves to prayer, being watchful and thankful."

— Colossians 4:2

Many people think there is a specific formula for praying, sort of like a math problem; plug your need into the equation and out comes the answer! Yet it's not always like this. Jesus hears the prayer of a scientific professor with intellectual vocabulary just as He hears every little three-year-old's prayer, too. The Bible says that Jesus sticks closer than a brother. If He's even closer than a family member, that should give you comfort in sharing your thoughts. Prayer is really just talking to God like He's your best friend. If someone doesn't know what to pray, there's always something to be thankful for (just like this verse in Colossians compels us to be thankful). God listens to our prayers, our cries for help, and our expressions of thankfulness.

PRAYER: Dear Lord, I want to pray more often and also listen to Your voice. Please show me the power of prayer. Amen.

notes:

PEOPLE PAY ATTENTION

"Don't have anything to do with foolish and stupid arguments, because you know they will produce quarrels."

— *2 Timothy 2:23*

I have the tendency to be stubborn and highly opinionated about a lot of things. Most of them truly don't matter. Who cares if I see white and gold when everyone else sees blue and black (for anyone who remembers "the dress" challenge on Facebook). What's most important is that those around us, especially people who aren't Christians, see love, kindness, and patience demonstrated even if there is a disagreement. On every form of social media, it's not hard to find an intense debate between a Christian and someone who's not a Christian. While our main goal should be to tell others about Christ, our witness fails when we stoop to insulting others. Whether you like it or not, people pay attention when you get upset and note how you respond. Ask God to give you the words to speak in hard moments.

PRAYER: God, I pray that You would forgive me for the times I have shown hate rather than Your love. Please give me wisdom in what to say, and please give me patience in how I act. Amen.

ALL OR NOTHING

"Love the Lord your God with all your heart and with all your soul and with all your mind and with all your strength."

— *Mark* 12:30

There are tons of different ways people can show love. People get famous by expressing their love through songs or get on the bestseller's list by writing about love. The phrase, "All or nothing" sums up a huge part of Christianity. However you choose to show your love to God, go all out! Just as we shouldn't half-heartedly love Jesus, He is not capable of partly loving us. When His children make mistakes, He doesn't partly forgive, or secretly keep a record of wrongs. Honestly, what is a human without his or her heart, soul, mind, and strength? Nothing! Jesus is calling you to love God with all that you have and all that you are. Don't let Him go to your voicemail.

PRAYER: Dear Lord, thank You so much for loving me. Show me how I can fully love You without holding back. Amen.

notes:

HE GIVES US THE WORDS

"Whenever you are arrested and brought into trial, do not worry beforehand about what to say. Just say whatever is given to you at the time, for it is not you speaking, but the Holy Spirit."

— *Mark* 13:11

The state of Michigan requires every sophomore in high school to learn about the theory of evolution. When I was a sophomore, I felt very convicted listening to what I didn't believe in. So with the help of a few friends, I presented the view of creationism to five biology classes in my public high school. I'm not going to lie . . . it was probably the scariest thing I've ever done. Yet, I believe that the verse above fit my situation perfectly. I didn't know how everything was going to turn out, but the Holy Spirit was with me, giving me the words to speak. Though you may not get "arrested" like Paul or other followers of Jesus, times will come when your faith will be questioned. Always choose to trust in the guidance of the Holy Spirit!

PRAYER: Holy Spirit, thank You for Your presence. Thank You for filling me with the right things to say. Help me to lean on You. Amen.

"I didn't know how everything was going to turn out, but the Holy Spirit was with me, giving me the words to speak."

TAKE OUT THE PLANK

"Therefore, my brothers, I want you to know that through Jesus the forgiveness of sins is proclaimed to you."

— *Acts 13:38*

Let's face it—everyone in this world is pretty quick to recognize the wrongdoings of those around him or her! Yet, what about their own faults? It's so easy for me to be judgmental when I still have things in my life that need cleaning up. Matthew 7:5 reads, "You hypocrite, first take the plank out of your own eye, and then you will see clearly to remove the speck from your brother's eye." As I get older, I am learning just how much I truly need God. Without Him, I am nothing. I fail daily. I can doubt Him in times of trouble, and my pride is a wall that gets in the way. But that's why we need Jesus. If life was perfect and no one made mistakes, we wouldn't be human! The name of Jesus is meant for us to rely on, as He forgives us time after time. People definitely have their annoyances, and Jesus gets to deal with seven billion of them—with care! Ask for His wisdom and guidance when facing temptations. God will help you.

PRAYER: Jesus, let me never lose the wonder of who You are and what You've done for me. I pray that I would learn to forgive others just as You have forgiven me. Amen.

DAY 52

IS ANYTHING TOO HARD?

"Then the Lord said to Abraham, 'Why did Sarah laugh and say, "Will I really have a child, now that I am old?"' **Is anything too hard for the Lord?"**

— *Genesis 18:13–14a*

This is such a cool story in the Bible. Could you imagine a 90-year-old woman giving birth? That is truly a sign of God's miracles! Sarah, Abraham's wife, did not have an entirely smooth journey. This verse shares that she doubted God. A lot of people may assume that the characters in the Bible are perfect (and that all God does is get angry). That is not true! He graciously extends His love to us, just as He did to Sarah when she gave birth to Isaac. The Bible contains stories of real people with real problems. Still, God is at work in the middle of it all. In Genesis 21:1 it says, "The Lord did for Sarah what He had promised."

PRAYER: Dear Lord, I don't ever want to doubt You and Your power. Help me to be faithful to You just as You're faithful in fulfilling Your promises. Amen.

notes:

SAY YES TO THE ONE

"Whoever finds his life will lose it, and whoever loses his life for my sake will find it."

— *Matthew* 10:39

Christianity is a paradox. There's no way to understand everything God has set up. In a way, that's another reason to praise Him because He is capable of the unimaginable! How could someone possibly find his or her life and lose it at the same time? Matthew 10:39 explains that in order to find your life in God, you'll need to give up your time, your decisions, and who you are for Him. The least we can do is say "yes" to the One who gave His life . . . so we didn't have to. Losing your life means disregarding what the world says is needed. If you follow Jesus, people should be able to tell by your words and actions that your life belongs to Him. Jesus is the Way, the Truth, and the Life. Truly, there's no life without Him.

PRAYER: Dear Jesus, remind me that as a Christian I should fully devote my life to You. Let me lay aside everything that is holding me back. I love You. Amen.

notes:

LOOK FOR THE MOMENTS

"If your enemy is hungry, feed him; if he is thirsty, give him something to drink."

— *Romans 12:20*

Helping the needy and homeless, or visiting someone in the hospital, is something everyone would consider a good deed. You don't have to go on a mission trip out of the country to help others or to experience an encounter with God. (This doesn't mean you shouldn't do that, but that you should first be able to witness to those in your daily life.) Maybe God's simple mission for you in one day is to speak kind words to someone, being intentional about loving that person. Feed people with kindness! This verse isn't just restricted to food and water. While Jesus was being persecuted, He said to God, "Forgive them, for they don't know what they're doing." Look for moments today to be an encouragement to someone else, whether it's by what you say or what you do.

PRAYER: Dear God, I want to show Your love to all people— whether I like them or not. My mission field is right here, where You've placed me. Thank You, Father. Amen

DAY 55

PEOPLE MATTER

"The second is this: 'Love your neighbor as yourself.'"

— *Mark* 12:31

Honesty time . . . I don't always live up to the expectations of this verse. I can easily think of a hundred things I do for myself in just one day. In this section of Scripture, Jesus is sharing that Christians are to rise above the mentality of "me, myself, and I. "Truthfully, I don't think this world is going to make it any easier, but I am not living for this world! I'm sold out for Jesus. While the majority of young people constantly focus on glorifying themselves and increasing the number of followers they have on Instagram, I challenge you to be bold and stand out! Stand out by noticing what people care about. Stand out by taking the time to truly listen to others. When it comes down to it, none of your "stuff" matters; people matter, and they're all around you.

PRAYER: Dear God, sometimes it's hard to remember that I need to love other people like I love myself. Please help me to not get caught up in pride and self-centeredness. Instead, I want to love others like You love me. Amen.

PURITY MATTERS

"Treat younger men as brothers, older women as mothers, and younger women as sisters, with absolute purity."

— 1 Timothy 5:2

Absolute purity is an important component that is decreasing in the world more and more each day. Modesty has been disregarded for self-expression. But I believe it doesn't have to be one or the other! A guy will treat a girl based on how she expresses herself. Ladies, if you set your standards high and make your morals known, there won't be a question about how a man should treat you. This might mean searching extra hard to find clothes that actually aren't skimpy. (Believe me, I know the struggle.) Guys, if you start out by keeping a good relationship with your mom, that will translate to your future relationships with women! Women will know how you will treat them in the future just by looking at how you treat others now, especially your family. However, when you have a solid relationship with Jesus Christ, it makes it possible for other relationships to be solid, too.

PRAYER: Dear Lord, I pray that who I am would exemplify purity. Help me to think and act in a pure way. I want to always keep my relationship with You a priority. Amen.

"Absolute purity is an important component that is decreasing in the world more and more each day. Modesty has been disregarded for self-expression. But I believe it doesn't have to be one or the other."

DAY 57

REFUGE AND REWARDS

"May the Lord repay you for what you have done. May you be richly rewarded by the Lord, the God of Israel, under whose wings you have come to take refuge."

— *Ruth* 2:12

These words were spoken by Boaz, a man who told Ruth that he really respected the fact that she went to live with her husband's mom when Ruth's husband died. Little did Ruth know that the man speaking this blessing over her would soon marry her! I think this story reminds us to always do the right thing—you never know who could be watching. It also shows that we should hold out for love. I'm sure after Ruth's husband died, she had very little hope in finding happiness, but God can restore! If you haven't found your special someone, remember that God has the perfect one in store for you—in His time. (However, He has occasionally called some people to be single . . . Paul, for example.) Who says the Bible is boring? It has cute love stories!

PRAYER: Jesus, I pray that we wouldn't limit Boaz's blessing to Ruth. Let us have the desire in our own lives to be richly rewarded by You. We want to take refuge under Your wings. Amen.

DAY 58

DON'T SWEAT THE SMALL STUFF

"Then Jesus said to his disciples: 'Therefore I tell you, do not worry about your life, what you will eat; or about your body, what you will wear. Life is more than food, and the body more than clothes.'"

— *Luke* 12:22–23

One busy day, I was just moving through life when I was struck by a few words someone said: "Don't sweat the small stuff." It is so easy for me to get worked up about what clothes I don't have, what clothes I can't find, what clothes don't fit. The list goes on and on. But Jesus calls us to spend our time thinking of more valuable things. (Still, isn't it crazy how this verse is relatable 2,000 years later? Jesus knew that you would eventually read it and need it.) In the grand scheme of things, what you're worried about today, you possibly won't remember a year from now. Let go . . . and let God! So, the next time you're last in line, you don't get the food you want, or if you're convinced you have nothing to wear, remember to count the blessings God has given you.

PRAYER: Dear God, help me to be grateful for what You've done and what You've given me. I pray that I would give my trust to You. Amen.

DAY
59

HUMBLE YOURSELF IN WORSHIP

"Ezra praised the Lord, the great God; and all the people lifted their hands and responded, 'Amen! Amen!' Then they bowed down and worshiped the Lord with their faces to the ground."

— Nehemiah 8:6

There are a few aspects from the Bible times that are undoubtedly outdated: fashion, transportation, and of course their lack of iphonography! What is not outdated is God's power. He is still worthy to be praised after all these years! Lifting your hands to Jesus can be a sign of surrender to Him. It's a way of saying, "Yes, Jesus!" or "I need You!" Worship can also be expressed in many forms for different people. Maybe you feel closest to God when you're taking a walk. That can be a form of worship. I know a form of worshiping for me is glorifying God through running. Worship is a way of humbling yourself before the Lord—when life is going great and when it's falling apart.

PRAYER: Dear Jesus, show me the way You want me to worship You. I want to draw closer to who You are, God. Amen.

notes:

DAY 60

HOW'S YOUR HEART?

**"Above all else, guard your heart,
for it is the wellspring of life."**

— *Proverbs 4:23*

Growing up, I have heard the words, "guard your heart" quite a lot from my grandma (Grandma Glory) and my mom. Even as a senior in high school, I had never been in a dating relationship with a boy. But I'm not here to tell you that is the way everyone should live. I think this verse simply means: hold out for God's best for you. Perhaps "His best" is not in high school or even college. I once heard from a pastor that "singleness is a gift." I had never looked at it from that perspective until I heard those words. God has you in each specific season of your life for a reason. Don't glorify a relationship with the opposite sex more than you glorify your relationship with God. The condition of your heart is not something you should take lightly. Trust God and His timing.

PRAYER: Dear Jesus, sometimes thinking about dating relationships is hard. You see my future. I pray that You would give me wisdom in the choices I make. Amen.

"I had once heard from a pastor
that 'singleness is a gift.'
I had never looked at it from
that perspective until
I heard those words."

"They claim to know God, but by their actions they deny him. They are detestable, disobedient, and unfit for doing anything good."

— Titus 1:16

In today's culture, I have heard a lot of drama about people being called "fake." It can upset others if a person acts one way to please friends, and then he or she acts differently to please another set of friends. Well, God can relate! He doesn't like it when people are fakes, either! It is one thing to know of God. It's a very different thing to know Him. Don't let your knowledge of God come from wavering, unreliable or convenient sources. That's like betting your life on the ending message in the game of Telephone! Dig deep into the Bible and discover things for yourself. How could you know everything entailed in being a Christian without reading the Bible? Make sure your words and actions reflect God's Word. Let the Holy Spirit guide and direct you.

PRAYER: Dear God, teach me to follow You well and follow You all the time. I don't want to be a "fake" Christian. Give me wisdom as I make decisions in life. I love You. Amen.

THE GIFT OF GRACE

**"But to each one of us grace has been given
as Christ apportioned it."**

— Ephesians 4:7

The word "testimony" is spoken frequently wherever there's a steeple or an Amen! I have never known what to share when asked about my testimony. I have been a Christian for as long as I can remember, being a pastor's kid. I don't have a story about an amazing turnaround, but what I do have is grace. We all have grace. Sometimes I think about what I would say or do if Jesus never came into my life. Those are moments when I realize who I would be; the sinner I am is saved by who Jesus is. He gave us all the gift of grace along with mercy when we have done nothing to deserve it. Imagine if God had the patience of the average young person . . . there would be quite a lot of hateful tweets! People mess up, but God never does.

PRAYER: Dear Jesus, I thank You so much for Your grace. No matter what my testimony is, You have still thought of me. Help me to show grace to others, too. Amen.

notes:

TRY GIVING HIM GLORY

"Pharaoh said to Joseph, 'I had a dream, and no one can interpret it. But I have heard it said of you that when you hear a dream, you can interpret it.' 'I cannot do it,' Joseph replied to Pharaoh, 'but God will give Pharaoh the answer he desires.'"

— Genesis 41:15–16

Joseph's humility is simply amazing. Imagine being sold by your brothers into slavery, being falsely accused of attempting to make advances toward an official's wife, and being put in prison. Joseph still trusted God after all of that. He chose to give God the glory when Pharaoh was complimenting him. This reminds me to not be so focused on myself in life. The next time someone compliments you for doing a task well, try giving the glory to God. All of our gifts and talents really do come from Him. The little things we stress about in life are so small compared to what Joseph went through. If the Lord has a plan for him, He has a plan for you!

PRAYER: Father, I want to remember that life is not all about me. Help me to give the glory to You and give my worries to You, also. Amen.

DAY
64

VALUE EACH PERSON

"Be merciful to those who doubt."

— Jude 1:22

Those six words are so powerful. Sometimes I think the Church can get so caught up in apologetics and politics that it forgets to love. Don't get me wrong . . . it is absolutely important to know what you believe. It is also important to develop relationships. It crushes me when I see Christians being rude to nonbelievers on social media. In the times when talking isn't effective, prayer always is. This is my point: Jesus did not come to Earth to create little bubbles of Christians that cannot be popped. Love everyone! You don't have to compromise your beliefs to have respect for someone else. The value of each person is more significant than the mistakes he or she has made. Always show mercy and always show the love of Jesus.

PRAYER: Dear God, please tell me the right moments to speak and the right moments to be quiet. I want to be humble and show grace to others. Amen.

notes:

STRONGER IN THE STRUGGLES

"Indeed, in our hearts we felt the sentence of death.
But this happened that we might not rely on ourselves
but on God, who raises the dead."

— 2 Corinthians 1:9

One of the biggest questions asked about life is why bad things happen to good people. I can honestly say that some of the strongest Christians I know have gone through a lot. Why? God made them stronger amidst their struggles. My friend, Reyna, explained to me that if you went to school and were never tested, it may be more fun, but you wouldn't learn as much. It's the same way in life! Jesus is the ultimate teacher—He doesn't solely throw curveballs at us, but He also leads us on the right path. In this chapter of 2 Corinthians, Paul describes how he experienced extreme suffering while recognizing that the main purpose of suffering was to draw him closer to God.

PRAYER: Lord, sometimes I don't understand everything that goes on in my life. I pray that I would trust You and rely on You. Amen.

notes:

OPEN THE GIFT

"For God did not send his Son into the world to condemn the world, but to save the world through him."

— *John 3:17*

This verse might be surprising to people who haven't heard of it! God is so much more than someone who corrects others when they are wrong. Anyone can do that! Jesus truly is the only One who can save. How does it feel to have someone correct you if they don't know you that well? It's easier to receive constructive criticism if that person has shown that he or she cares. Well, it's 100 percent certain that Jesus cares about you. He also wants the best for you. Take the time to invest in and develop your relationship with Jesus Christ. Without Jesus, I personally believe I would be mean, proud, judgmental, and insecure. Don't leave the gift of eternal life in a gift box to sit and get dusty. Get some use out of that gift while Jesus uses you for His glory.

PRAYER: Dear Lord, I pray that I would recognize all that You have done. Thank You so much for saving me. My life wouldn't be the same without You. Amen.

notes:

"It's 100 percent certain that Jesus cares about you. He also wants the best for you. Take the time to invest in and develop your relationship with Jesus Christ."

DAY 67

GOD RESTORES AND PROVIDES

"You intended to harm me, but God intended it for good to accomplish what is now being done, the saving of many lives."

— *Genesis 50:20*

A Bible character, Joseph, spoke these words to his brothers after they sold him as a slave. They sold him into slavery to get rid of him. I don't know about you, but I would be a little ticked off at my three older siblings if they sold me into slavery (don't get any ideas Autumn, Jonathan, and Victoria)! If you aren't familiar with this story, Joseph's older brothers sold him because they were jealous of how much their dad, Jacob, liked him. The brothers put blood from an animal on Joseph's coat, and then told Jacob that Joseph was dead. (Who needs reality TV when you can just read the Bible?) So, fast-forward many years, and Joseph is well respected in a high position in Egypt, where he was first sold as a slave. God restored the relationship he had with his family. Instead of holding a grudge, Joseph recognized the fact that God used him in mighty ways to help a lot of people because of what his brothers did. Allow the Lord to use your trial—your bondage in "slavery," whatever it is—for greater things today.

PRAYER: God, the next time I am going through something rough, help me to remember how You have provided for so many people before. You never fail to be my Provider. Amen.

notes:

GRACE AND HOLINESS

"If we confess our sins, he is faithful and just and will forgive us our sins and purify us from all unrighteousness."

— 1 John 1:9

Sometimes, I think the word "sin" can freak people out. It all comes down to this: no one is perfect, but God still forgives us. This doesn't mean, however, that we can apologize to God for doing wrong and then automatically start sinning again. When I saw the public speaker/preacher, Christine Caine, she said that "Grace doesn't exclude holiness." This really struck a chord with me, because Christians should not use God's grace as an excuse in their everyday lives. This verse shares that God will "purify us from all unrighteousness." That sounds pretty good to me! One thing I am so thankful about being a Christian is that I don't have to spend my life wondering if someone will accept me. Jesus doesn't always accept our actions, but He does accept us all as His sons and daughters. When we ask, He washes away our dark sin so it doesn't cloud our view of Him.

PRAYER: Dear Jesus, thank You for always loving me, even when I mess up. Help me to ask for forgiveness when I need it. Thank You for Your faithfulness. Amen.

DAY 69

A QUIET LIFE

"Make it your ambition to lead a quiet life, to mind your own business and to work with your hands, just as we told you, so that your daily life may win the respect of outsiders and so that you will not be dependent on anybody."

— I Thessalonians 4:11-12

What does it mean to lead a quiet life? In my opinion, it doesn't mean shying away from sharing the gospel. Instead, it's living the gospel—drawing attention to God instead of you. While talking to some friends about humility, I was reminded to let my actions speak louder than my words. That is what these two verses are all about! There is no need to fear what other people are thinking; there is no need to compare yourself to others. You'll gain respect when you don't try to be someone you are not. Fashions and fads come and go. What is cool and "in" right now will never compare to eternal life! Turn your focus to God and what He has for you. Make His name famous in everything you do and that's when you'll be living a "quiet" life!

PRAYER: Lord, I pray that my daily life and the things I do would lead others to You. Help me to live a life of humility, and help me to work hard to bring You praise. Amen.

CARRY YOUR OWN LOAD

"Each one should test his own actions. Then he can take pride in himself, without comparing himself to somebody else, for each one should carry his own load."

— *Galatians 6:4–5*

One thing I can definitely work on in my Christian faith is judgment. It's easy to judge others without thinking about it, but I have no right to! In God's eyes, each sin is looked at the same way. The verse above shares that we all need to look at our own hearts before we start condemning others. Frankly, you can't fix your own life by only telling others what to do. Take action and "carry your own load." I feel that a lot of times judgment leads to self-criticism. If you are jealous of someone, odds are you're finding something to judge about them. This is not the way God intended it to be! Let's cooperate together to share the love of Jesus instead of spreading hate.

PRAYER: Lord, You see my heart and my thoughts. I pray that You would teach me to follow in Your footsteps—not trying to fit my foot into someone else's shoe! Amen.

notes:

"Frankly, you can't fix your own life by only telling others what to do. Take action and carry your own load."

"Wealth and honor come from you; you are the ruler of all things. In your hands are strength and power to exalt and give strength to all."

— 1 Chronicles 29:12

For many millennials, they pay money to go to school so they can get a job, which gives them money, so they can spend more money. That's a lot of cash! I am far from a financial expert—I mean really far—but I imagine that it could get tiring chasing after money. That's why David, who prayed the verse above, totally surrendered his life to God. Maybe you don't know where your next meal will come from; maybe God has blessed you abundantly with your finances. Either way, it's comforting to know that God's wealth is so much greater than any type of currency this world can create! True wealth and honor are rooted in God with integrity. God is in control, so ask Him for wisdom and trust Him in all aspects.

PRAYER: Dear Lord, it can be easy to get caught up in the worries of money. I want to remember that You bring me true wealth. Thank You for all the ways You have blessed me. Amen.

notes:

DAY
12

TRUSTING IN A GOD WHO KNOWS YOU

"In God I trust; I will not be afraid. What can man do to me?"

— *Psalm* 56:11

In order for one person to gain another's trust, he has to constantly prove himself. Trust also requires a relationship. You would never ask a hitchhiker to hold $500 for you, or pick a random stranger to take care of your children. There are several qualities to look for in a trustworthy person: empathy, wisdom, and honesty. It's safe to say that God takes the cake in all of those areas! One of my favorite songs called "You Know Me" by Bethel Music says, "Nothing is hidden from Your sight. Wherever I go, You'll find me. You know every detail from my life. You are God, and You don't miss a thing." God loves knowing all the small details about you. He knows what causes you to fear, and He knows how to protect you. God allows trials to make us stronger, but when we fall, He is there. He walks with us and even helps us as we get back up. So trust in God. What can man do to you?

PRAYER: Dear Jesus, I pray that You would call me out when I do not fully trust You. There is no One more deserving and worthy of my trust than You. Amen.

FAITH THAT CAN MOVE CARS FROM DITCHES

"I have fought the good fight, I have finished the race, I have kept the faith."

— *2 Timothy 4:7*

One of the best feelings is completing a hard task, like getting 100 percent on a test you studied hard for, or finishing a race with every ounce of energy you have left. You want to know what else is a hard task? Life. There are days when it feels like you're running forever and your finish line isn't in sight. For example, one winter evening, I was running late to an event, got my car stuck in a ditch, and got a flat tire, all in a matter of three hours! In tough moments, choose to turn to God, and keep the faith. One thing I love about the Bible is that it does not sugarcoat; it's not fake. Christ-followers really went through some tough stuff! Paul, the man who wrote this verse, spent time in prison for following Jesus. Yet, he still knew that the fight was worth fighting. Why? Well, the next verse goes on to say that the crown of righteousness is in store in Heaven. Keep fighting, keep running, and keep the faith.

PRAYER: Lord, show me how I can fight for You and Your will. I want to be strong for whatever life brings me. Give me perseverance and strength as I live for You. Amen.

ANNOYING ANNOYANCES

**"A fool shows his annoyance at once,
but a prudent man overlooks an insult."**

— *Proverbs* 12:16

There's no doubt that teenagers—or just people in general—like to talk about their annoyances. If you scroll on someone's Twitter feed, there are likely to be twice as many negative tweets as positive tweets. (Even though I don't have a Twitter, I'm preaching to myself, too!) It seems as if our generation has realized that more attention is given to them if their social media post allows them to use the "annoyed emoji." However, this Bible verse is a reminder to let life's little irritations roll off your back. People will fail you. But God is a good God, and there's always something to be thankful for. Spread the love, not bitterness!

PRAYER: Dear God, it can be so easy to rant on and on about what's bothering me. I pray that You would replace those negative words with words of joy. Teach me how to be patient in hard moments. Amen.

notes:

HEALING WITH FAITH

"Paul looked directly at him, saw that he had faith to be healed and called out, 'Stand up on your feet!' At that, the man jumped up and began to walk."

— *Acts 14:9b–10*

Aren't God's miracles so amazing? Imagine never being able to walk your entire life, then with five simple words, the gift of mobility was given to you by the power of Jesus. Here's one thing to take away from this story: the lame man had faith. His faith was evident enough for Paul to see. During the end of my track season of my sophomore year in high school, I had an unexpected injury. It was very minor, but it came at the most inconvenient time—the week before the state meet. I remember sitting in my room with my mom and brother, just crying out to God for healing. I don't think I've ever prayed that hard for anything before (by God's grace, I was still able to get All-State honors in the mile and two-mile at my state meet)! That prayer started with my mom comforting me and calling on Jesus, just as Paul did for the lame man. Always remember: Jesus is the greatest Healer.

PRAYER: Dear God, please remind me that miracles aren't restricted to Bible stories, but that they can happen in my life today. I never want to be afraid to cry to You for healing. Amen.

THE LORD'S BLESSING

"Blessed is she who has believed that what the Lord has said to her will be accomplished."

— *Luke* 1:45

This verse is so cool! If you have faith in the Lord, you will receive His blessings. I also like the fact that it uses the word, "she!" Elizabeth spoke these words to Mary before she gave birth to Jesus. (Side note: could you imagine carrying Jesus—God's perfect Son—in your womb (if you are a female)? I would feel even guiltier about my eating habits!) Mary probably got a lot of hate from people who didn't understand her situation. After all, Mary was blessed with a baby without Joseph and before their marriage! Talk about drama! Yet, the *Fire Bible* states, "She willingly accepted the honor and criticism that being Jesus's mother would bring." Mary had to tell herself that God was in control. You probably won't be experiencing anything as crazy as being the mother to the Savior of the world! Declare today that you will have faith in the Lord. He can do all things!

PRAYER: Lord, I want to know how I can trust You better. You are so good, and You work all things together for my good. I love You. Amen.

"Lord, I want to know how I can trust You better. You are so good, and You work all things together for my good."

DAY
11

FRIENDSHIP GOALS

"My command is this: Love each other as I have loved you. Greater love has no one than this, that he lay down his life for his friends."

— John 15:12–13

Love. It's what everyone wants. It is the perceived outward appearance of "relationship goals" and "friendship goals." Yet, people are looking for the root of love in the wrong places. The only way you can fully and truly love another person is through God's love. I think it's time for "friendship goals" to be of building one another up and having integrity. Love is much deeper than sending kissy emojis back and forth. Really try to be a friend to someone who needs it today! Jesus was and is the ultimate Best Friend. The verse above says that a friend should lay down his life for others, and that's exactly what He did! He also commanded us to replicate His love in our every-day lives. In other words, we should lay down our lives for our friends. Try dying to yourself in order to put others first. Be real and really love people today.

PRAYER: Dear Jesus, thank You so much for the love You showed by dying for me. Let me love others and be a good friend to them. Amen.

PROVE YOUR TRUST

"In him we were also chosen, having been predestined according to the plan of him who works out everything in conformity with the purpose of his will."

— *Ephesians* 1:11

You. You were predestined by God. Before you were created. Before you took your first breath. God chose you. How cool is that? Never ever believe the lie that you are worthless. Take time to love yourself. Sometimes it's easier to love other people because you don't hold their flaws to the same standard as yours. Today can be the day when that ends. You have so much potential! Even if you don't understand your life right now, this verse reminds us that God works everything out for the purpose of His will. When a friend opened up to me about her anxiety, I told her to "prove to God that you trust Him." The next day, I found myself needing my own advice! So, never think that you're not good enough. Believe God when He says that you are valuable . . . you always have been and you always will be.

PRAYER: Lord, remind me that I was predestined by You on the days that my confidence is low. Thank You for loving me unconditionally. Amen.

DAY 19

WEAKNESS IS STRENGTH

"That is why, for Christ's sake, I delight in weaknesses, in insults, in hardships, in persecutions, in difficulties. For when I am weak, then I am strong."

— 2 Corinthians 12:10

This is my most favorite verse in the Bible, which some people may call their "life verse." I remember quoting this to my sister at the starting line of our regional meet before our cross-country race. I believe it gave me strength to persevere through tough moments. Through God's help, I came in first that day and so did my team. But that moment was so much bigger than winning—it was about trusting God that He cared about the little things I cared about, too. What is an area in your life that you need to learn how to trust God better? It is really easy to declare to God, "Spirit, lead me where my trust is without borders," and then put up borders when the going gets tough. (Been there. Done that.) Delight in your weaknesses, because with Jesus, there is always hope. He is making you strong.

PRAYER: Jesus, when my life is hard, show me that You're making me strong. Teach me how to delight in difficulties so I can trust You more. Amen.

THE GREATEST WEAPON OF ALL

"David said to the Philistine, 'You come against me with sword and spear and javelin, but I come against you in the name of the Lord Almighty, the God of the armies of Israel, whom you have defied.'"

— 1 Samuel 17:45

The story of David and Goliath is one of the most famous stories in the Bible. Maybe you've heard it countless times. But it is famous for a reason! When David fought Goliath, all the odds were stacked against him. He was much, much smaller than Goliath. He didn't have the "best" equipment for fighting, and he had a lot less experience. What made the difference was that David declared out loud that his strength came from the Lord. Think about it . . . David was fighting for some pretty major reasons—it was literally life or death. The next time you face a giant in life, remember that it all starts with your decision to declare your strength in the name of the Lord, Jesus.

PRAYER: Dear God, I pray that I can learn from David's experience for my own life. I want to have faith in You, even before I face my battles. Amen.

notes:

"The next time you face a giant in your life, remember that it all starts with your decision to declare your strength in the name of the Lord, Jesus."

SOMETHING TO BE THANKFUL FOR

**"Give thanks to the Lord, for he is good;
his love endures forever."**

— *Psalm* 118:1

We really do serve a good God. He is pretty incredible. In fact, He died for you so that you could have eternal life! What could be more special than that? He also loves us. God isn't just some random being giving orders to the little people He knows nothing about. He knows you and will love you forever. Nothing else lasts forever but Him. People can freak out about clothes and sports and relationships, but those things only last a lifetime (which is nothing close to forever). God is so cool, because we can't even comprehend all of who He is and what He is capable of. I believe the focus of our prayers needs to change from "Give me" to "Thank You." God's blessings are abundant. They're overflowing. A blessing could be something small, like a good grade on a quiz. It could be something huge, like a financial gift. Whatever it is, remember that there's always something to be thankful for.

PRAYER: Father, You are a big God, capable of big things. I want to thank You for what You have done in my life and what You will do. I love You, Lord. Amen.

STRONGER THAN YESTERDAY

"I know your deeds, your love and faith, your service and perseverance, and that you are now doing more than you did at first."

— Revelation 2:19

My old youth pastor, Dave Borowsky, said that you know you have grown in your faith if you are closer to God now than you were a year ago. There are days when I fall short with my relationship with God. It's easy to be lazy with my Bible reading, or even just caring for other people, but I know I need to put in the work to keep a strong relationship with Christ! So, are you obeying the Lord more than you did at first? Of course, no one can be a perfect Christian. John (the man who wrote the book of Revelation) goes on to say that the church he is writing to has to clean up their act! Just remember that you don't have to let your past mistakes keep you from doing what is right today. Have love, faith, perseverance, and challenge yourself to be better than you ever have been before.

PRAYER: Dear Lord, I want to be active in my relationship with You. Give me Your eyes and ears so I can learn how to follow You more. Amen.

LIVING BY THE SPIRIT, NOT SOCIAL MEDIA

"So I say, live by the Spirit, and you will not gratify the desire of the sinful nature (the flesh)."

— *Galatians 5:16 (ESV)*

I am going to be honest here: I think part of me can be addicted to social media. Maybe you are, too. It happens without realizing it. Five minutes becomes an hour, which can become two hours. And what are we spending our time doing as we scroll? We are judging others. We are being jealous and envious. We are paying attention to the number of followers we have to evaluate our self-worth. I don't know about you, but I don't want social media to define me or destroy me. And if I allow it to happen, it will. Now, social media itself is not evil, but there are a lot of evil things that can come out of it. So, what can be done to resist temptation? Stay deep in God's Word. Focus on what He has for you instead of which selfie to post! With any temptation, you can also set boundaries for yourself. For example, some friends and I take the month of February off of social media each year. It is amazing what can happen when you listen to the Holy Spirit instead of worldly desires.

PRAYER: Dear God, I don't want to waste my time by being tempted with the things of this world. Give me self-control as I live for You. Amen.

DAY
84

LOVE IS AN ACTION

**"If anyone has material possessions and sees his
brother in need, but has not pity on him,
how can the love of God be in him?"**

— 1 John 3:17

My friend Jillian once told me, "Clicking is not caring." She meant that you are not showing true love and empathy for someone just by liking a status or a picture online. This is true for many life situations as well. People can say a lot about what went wrong in their days, and the general tendency is to show sympathy for a few moments, and then move on. Love is an action. As Christians, it is our job to act upon it! But what few people realize, some of the best things we can do for a person are free—they just require a few seconds of your time. A few kind words or a brief note can transform someone's day! One time I wrote a note to a friend who I thought could use some encouragement. We weren't extremely close, but she told me that she almost teared up reading the note. Go out of your way to make someone else's day. Let the love of God burn brightly inside of you!

PRAYER: Dear God, I am sorry for the times I haven't cared enough about—or even noticed—the people around me. Let me love others the way You love me. Amen.

A JEALOUS GOD

"Do not worship any other god, for the Lord, whose name is jealous, is a jealous God."

— *Exodus 34:4*

I have heard the words, "He is jealous for me" or "God is a jealous God" many different times. However, I'm not sure how deeply I have looked into their true meaning. "Jealous" can be defined as "passionately protective." God is passionate about you! He is jealous when you spend your time with other people, especially when you're doing things that don't honor Him. He truly values you that much. This isn't saying that God will condemn you if every waking minute is not buried in your Bible. He just wants to be the top priority in your life. What are the steps you can take to make Him "Number One" in your life?

PRAYER: Lord, I don't want to have anything in my life that is more important than You. Remind me that You are jealous for Your children. Thank You for caring about me, even when I fail. Amen.

notes:

AN UMBRELLA IN THE STORM

**"Have I not commanded you? Be strong and courageous.
Do not be terrified; do not be discouraged, for the Lord
your God will be with you wherever you go."**

— *Joshua* 1:9

What is something that you never let leave your sight? Your phone? Wallet? Chapstick? Why is that? Because it shows that we value them. We want them around. God may not be in your physical sight, but He never leaves your side—and you don't even ask Him to be around! You don't have to put a ringer on Him in case of losing Him. The fact that God is always with us should give Christ-followers a bigger incentive to spread His message. When Jesus said, "Go and make disciples of all nations" (Matthew 28:19), do you really think He was planning for His followers to make disciples without any help? No way! My point is, there is literally nothing you could do to escape God's love for you. His comfort is an umbrella in a storm. His peace is a raft in the waves. His hope is a light in the night. Do not be discouraged. Be strong and courageous.

PRAYER: Father, thank You for never leaving my side. Let my fears fade in Your presence. Amen.

"There is literally nothing you could do to escape God's love for you. His comfort is an umbrella in a storm. His peace is a raft in the waves. His hope is a light in the night. Do not be discouraged. Be strong and courageous."

DAY 87

THE CALLING

"As a prisoner for the Lord, then, I urge you to live a life worthy of the calling you have received. Be completely humble and gentle; be patient, bearing one another in love."

— Ephesians 4:1–2

Imagine if you got a letter from Paul, a man who was totally on fire for God, while he was in prison. I think I would feel honored that he was spending his time locked up, thinking about my faith. His words would also probably have more meaning. It's as if whomever Paul was writing to (such as the people from Ephesus), had an obligation to live out what Paul could not. God has called each and every one of us to a similar task of telling others about Him, yet our journeys are all different. Live up to the weight of that task in what you say and do! The verse above says to love people around you and have patience with them. It's not an easy thing to do, but it is one step closer to living out the calling you have received.

PRAYER: Dear Jesus, thank You for loving me enough to place a calling on my life. Teach me how to show that love to the people around me. Amen.

DAY
88

**"Humility and the fear of the Lord bring
wealth and honor and life."**

— *Proverbs 22:4*

If there is one thing the typical teenager lacks, it is humility. Some people constantly think of others as trash to make themselves feel better. Others simply think of themselves as trash. (Side note: you are worth it. You have a purpose.) I think it's really important to have a balance between humility and confidence. You don't need to be cocky to believe in yourself. The verse above says that humility will bring wealth. That is so interesting to me! A lot of people are the opposite of humble because of their wealth. No matter how you're living on Earth, God has a mansion for us all in Heaven! Don't diss who God made you. Be bold for Him, using your talents to point glory to Him instead of yourself.

PRAYER: Lord, I want to be humble. I don't want to think too highly of myself. If I start to be overconfident in myself, I pray that You would steer my thoughts back to You. Thank You for all You have blessed me with. Amen.

notes:

"But whatever was to my profit I now consider loss for the sake of Christ. What is more, I consider everything a loss compared to the surpassing greatness of knowing Christ Jesus my Lord, for whose sake I have lost all things."

— *Philippians 3:7–8a*

There's something about the words "all things." They are quoted in some of the most well-known verses of the Bible . . . "I can do all things through Him" (Philippians 4:13) or "In all things God works for the good of those who love Him" (Romans 8:28). I think this is showing that there is no "halfway" in following Jesus. It's all or nothing! Saying that you have lost everything that was once considered a gain can be a bit confusing. Following Jesus can sometimes be a paradox. How can God be the Father, Son, and Holy Spirit all in one? If God created the Earth, who created God? How can someone be first and last at the same time? In many ways, God's style is the complete opposite of what the world accepts. Ask the Lord to show you how to look at the losses in your life as victories!

PRAYER: Dear God, please help me to remember that I may not understand everything as I follow You and learn more about You, but that's okay. Let Your will be done. Amen.

AN UNDIVIDED HEART

"I will give them an undivided heart and put a new spirit in them; I will remove from them their heart of stone and give them a heart of flesh."

— *Ezekiel* 11:19

It is so amazing how God can take one creation and literally make it fully new through His power! I need to be reminded daily to have a heart of flesh. I want to care for others whole-heartedly and have empathy. To do something wholeheart-edly is having an undivided heart. Maybe you know someone who has his or her heart scattered in a million different places! Their declared motives and morals don't always line up with their actions. Perhaps you know of someone who has a hard heart; he or she isn't open to the Bible's (or God's) point of view and their focus is on their own desires. Let God put a new spirit in you if these qualities are present in your life.

PRAYER: Father, I pray that my heart would only long for You. Put a new spirit in me so that Your love for others radiates through me. I love You! Amen.

notes:

"I need to be reminded daily to have a heart of flesh. I want to care for others wholeheartedly and have empathy."

ASK. BELIEVE. RECEIVE.

"Therefore, I tell you, whatever you ask for in prayer, believe that you have received it, and it will be yours."

— *Mark* 11:24

If the status of your prayer life was the first thing everyone found out about you, how would you feel? Honestly, I might be a bit ashamed. Prayer is different than going to church and reading your Bible. It's personal. If we don't personally take the time to pray to God, how can we expect to grow spiritually? Growing up, my mom would tell me, "Feed your spirit man." She was saying that our souls hunger for more of God. You must keep your spiritual cravings fed instead of bingeing on a holiday and starving yourself when the going gets tough. Prayer takes faith. Faith takes patience. Patience takes strength. Don't let unsure moments in life slip away without a prayer . . . or ten!

PRAYER: Dear Jesus, give me the desire to pray to You daily, constantly, and to have faith while doing it. Amen.

notes:

DAY
92

TRUST GOD'S TIMING

**"There is a time for everything, and a season for
every activity under heaven."**

— *Ecclesiastes* 3:1

Have you ever had the post-holiday blues? Maybe you had an extended time where you didn't have any responsibilities, and then reality bluntly smacked you in the face. Or maybe you are going through a lot of life changes in a short period of time. When I was younger, I had four different schooling situations within five years. Change is hard! However, each transition and situation taught me specific things and shaped me to be who I am today. Our life situations may fluctuate, but God always stays constant. If you are waiting for God to answer a prayer, keep your hope in Him. Ask the Lord to give you wisdom with challenging decisions and changing situations.

PRAYER: God, please help me to trust You with Your timing. It's not always easy when I don't understand it. Give me patience when I need it and a flexible heart through transitions. I love You, Lord. Amen.

notes:

DAY 93

YOUR FAVORITE PAIR OF SHOES

**"For he is the living God and he endures forever;
his kingdom will not be destroyed,
his dominion will never end."**

— *Daniel 6:26b*

Think of your favorite pair of shoes. When you first got them, you probably wore them almost every day, right? You were so excited to show them off! After a while, your favorite shoes got worn out. Maybe you still wear them, scuff marks and all! Or maybe they have been shoved aside. You aren't ready to give them away because they have done you so much good in the past, but you aren't looking to bring them out any time soon. Sometimes, this is how people treat their lives with God. They are really excited for a season, but if things aren't as pretty as they once were, as the newness wears off, they put their faith on the back burner. This verse (spoken by King Darius after Daniel was in the lion's den) reminds us that God's power is everlasting!

PRAYER: Father, I pray that I never get lazy with my faith. I want to make You my biggest priority because Your love never changes and You last forever. Amen.

DO GOOD TO ALL

"Therefore, as we have opportunity, let us do good to all people, especially to those who belong in the family of believers."

— *Galatians 6:10*

Have you ever done that group activity where you write something nice for everyone in the room? Though I've experienced that exercise quite a few times, it never gets old to me. My mom has told me, "When you're sad, encourage someone else!" It's so true that doing good to others and being kind to them will make you happier, too! Since I am a girl, I get excited if someone compliments my hair or my shoes—it can be as simple as a few nice words. But it's not all about talking; it's about acting out. It's about doing things to further God's kingdom, not just to make yourself higher than others. Today you will have this opportunity—don't miss it.

PRAYER: Jesus, give me kind words to speak to other people and loving hands as I exemplify Your name. Thank You for being so good to me. Amen.

notes:

DAY
95

GOD HEARS YOUR CRY

**"Then you will call, and the Lord will answer;
you will cry for help and he will say: Here am I."**

— *Isaiah 58:9*

The difference between Adele calling her ex-boyfriend and you calling God is that when you say, "Hello, it's me," God actually replies. But seriously—it's really comforting to know that when tears stream down our faces, He is coming to our rescue. Sometimes prayers are answered instantly. Sometimes praying takes a lot of patience! Imagine that every hard decision or difficult situation is a puzzle piece. Don't try so hard to force your will when God has the perfect puzzle piece that will fit. (Cheesy, I know.) There's no one better to call on in times of desperation than Jesus Christ.

PRAYER: Dear Lord, show me that You're always there when I need Someone to lean on. Thank You for giving me Your wisdom and listening to my prayers. Amen.

notes:

A HEART AFTER GOD

**"I have hidden your word in my heart that
I might not sin against you."**

— *Psalm* 119:11

When I was a kid, I was the biggest fan of High School Musical. I either listened to Christian music, or Troy Bolton's voice as he serenaded millions of other little girls. Ten years later, if you asked me to sing along to the songs, I would probably know all of them! As Christians, this is how it should be with us and God's Word. Obviously, you're not going to memorize every verse in all 66 books of the Bible! But, today's verse does say to hide God's Word in your heart. Are you spending more time studying pop culture or the Word of God? Find a system for Bible reading and studying that works for you. Talk with friends about passages in the Bible. Write verses on notes to post around your house, in your locker, or at work. You will be able to face life's obstacles much more easily when your soul proclaims the Word of God!

PRAYER: Dear God, give me a heart that goes after You and Your Word. I pray that Your truth would be rooted deeply in me. Amen.

"Obviously, you're not going to memorize every verse in all 66 books of the Bible! But, today's verse does say to hide God's Word in your heart. Are you spending more time studying pop culture or the Word of God?"

DAY 97

HOLY SPIRIT COME

"God, who knows the heart, showed that he accepted them by giving the Holy Spirit to them, just as he did to us."

— *Acts* 15:8

Sometimes the entirety of the Holy Spirit can be hard to grasp. I am still learning a lot, too! I think it's cool that through the Holy Spirit, we can have an intimate relationship with God. Before Jesus died and rose again, people had to go to temples to encounter the presence of God. Do you realize that you don't even have to be in church to have a deep spiritual moment? God is literally everywhere. He is there when your adrenaline starts pumping before your sport. He is there during every test and every hard decision. He is there when you feel insecure about what other people are saying about you. After all, He knows your heart!

PRAYER: Lord, let me encounter Your presence in a new way. I don't want to forget that the Holy Spirit is always with me. Amen.

notes:

"Above all, my brothers, do not swear—not by heaven or by earth or anything else. Let your 'yes' be yes, and your 'no' no, or you will be condemned."

— *James 5:12*

This is a verse my parents have quoted to me several times! "Let your 'yes' be yes . . . " My life becomes really messy when I am preoccupied with unimportant things. I start to put off the things that really matter. I've had many "come to Jesus moments" when I told God I would stop doing a particular thing. But in those cases, my "yes" did not mean "yes." Even for simple matters, like when my parents have told me to do my homework or clean my room, it's tempting to shrug it off and say "okay" while I plan to watch another episode of Gilmore Girls. Of course, there are also times when God calls us to resist temptation and say, "no." Be a person who keeps your word.

PRAYER: Dear Jesus, I'm sorry for all the times I have not kept my word. Teach me to mean what I say and not throw my words around lightly. Amen.

notes:

DAY 99

BLESSED IS THE ONE WHO TRUSTS

"But blessed is the man who trusts in the Lord, whose confidence is in him."

— *Jeremiah 17:7*

Trusting in God is a lot easier said than done! I find myself trusting God when I'm worshipping at church, but I also want to trust Him during stressful moments in my daily life. Trusting means valuing your faith in Him rather than your worry. Our confidence to face life's hardships should not rely on ourselves. We're human. We mess up. That is why my confidence lies in God. He is perfect. He does not fail. At the end of your life, how wonderful would it be if God said to you, "You are blessed. You trusted in Me through some pretty hard times." This is a big way Jesus can relate to His followers. Jesus had to completely put His faith in God before He died on the cross. But amid the pain and struggle, He knew that His Father's plan was the best plan.

PRAYER: God, help me to trust You and place my confidence in You. You are worthy of all my praise. Amen.

notes:

OUT OF MY COMFORT ZONE

"I pray that you may be active in sharing your faith, so that you will have a full understanding of every good thing we have in Christ."

— *Philemon 1:6*

"Hide it under a bushel—no! I'm gonna let it shine! " That song may have been written for kids, but it's true for anyone at any age and any stage. This Scripture verse proclaims that you will understand life with Christ better when you share about your faith. The good news of Jesus was never meant to be kept quiet! Jesus is alive! Yes, sharing your faith with someone new (or even someone you already know) can be scary, but there is a first time for everything. Some of the most rewarding moments in my faith have been when I stepped out of my comfort zone to share His good news or simply by loving new friends.

PRAYER: Father, I want to have Your strength as I tell people about You and live my life to prove Your love to others. Thank You for giving me the words to say when I need them. Amen.

notes:

"Some of my most rewarding moments in my faith have been when I have stepped out of my comfort zone to share His good news or simply by loving new friends."

DAY
101

BE IMITATORS OF GOD

"Dear friend, do not imitate what is evil but what is good. Anyone who does what is good is from God. Anyone who does what is evil has not yet seen God."

— 3 John 1:11

Whether we admit to it or not, we are all imitators of someone! I find myself talking like my older sisters or my friends. Sometimes if you're around another person for a while, you'll pick up on their sayings. This is a reason why it's good to surround yourself with positive people who will lead you in the right direction. You can be that person for someone else! Do good deeds. Share Bible verses. Pray for people. Maybe they would start to imitate you. It really is a domino effect! The same goes for negative influences. Stay away from temptation by being rooted in His Word and choosing your friends wisely.

PRAYER: Dear Lord, I want to imitate only good things. Help me to steer away from evil and stay close to Your plan. Amen.

notes:

HOPE IN THE LORD

"The Lord is good to those whose hope is in him, to the one who seeks him; it is good to wait quietly for the salvation of the Lord."

— *Lamentations* 3:25–26

One day, I was with a group of friends, and someone said the words, "Guys, we're all gonna die someday!" Then they proceeded to talk about their fears that went along with death. Lightheartedly, I said, "I'm not scared because I know I'll see Jesus!" They answered, "I wish I had that reassurance," and laughed it off. While it may have been funny during the moment, it made me realize that there are people around us all who don't know what to place their hope in. I can testify that there are way too many distractions in this world—things that lead us in the wrong direction. As today's verse shares, take time to just be still in the presence of God! Have hope in the Lord and He will be good to you!

PRAYER: Dear God, show me how I can be an example of someone who has hope in You. Let me take my faith seriously and be quiet so I can hear Your voice. Amen.

notes:

DAY 103

KEEP NO RECORD OF WRONGS

"Blessed are the merciful for they will be shown mercy."

— *Matthew 5:7*

I'll be the first to admit that there are days when I'm stubborn, bossy, and closed-minded. It is easy to keep a mental note of the wrong things people have done. But Jesus doesn't keep a record of wrongs, so why should we? In high school, I walked right past someone talking badly about me. I remember crying to my mom about it, because it caused a lot of worry. It is always difficult when you experience criticism face-to-face, instead of behind your back. The person apologized to me, which gave me an opportunity to show them mercy! I could have held a grudge toward that person, but now I barely think about it. Words hurt. As hard as you try to shake them off, they could still be clinging on to you. Fill your life with the Word of God rather than words that will tear you down. Show grace and mercy—even to those who might have offended you, because God has shown grace and mercy to you!

PRAYER: Dear Lord, sometimes it is hard to forgive others and forget the things they've done wrong. Please teach me to love them. Amen.

DAY
104

THESE ARE THE DAYS!

**"Do not say, 'why were the old days better than these?'
For it is not wise to ask such questions."**

— *Ecclesiastes 7:10*

If there's any convicting verse in the Bible, it's this one! I love looking back at old memories, but sometimes I end up wishing my life was different than the way it is now. It's really true that you don't know what you have until it's gone! Cherish the people who are in your life. Be thankful for the small things. Appreciate your life now so you don't have to be sad about what you failed to appreciate later. In our Christian faith, it is easy to get pumped up about God after a big convention, missions trip, or camp. You can look back with a sigh saying, "Those were the days" or you can declare: "These are the days!" God is the same yesterday, today, and forever. He has the same power in a room full of a thousand people as when you're alone in your room. You might be going through stormy seas right now, but I promise, God, our Hope, is the Master of the seas, and He does not disappoint.

PRAYER: Dear Jesus, I am sorry for all of the times I have longed for the past instead of being grateful for the present or trusting You for the future. I want to have Your joy as I live my life. Amen.

DAY
105

PEACE ISN'T JUST FOR HIPPIES

"Lord, you establish peace for us; all that we have accomplished you have done for us."

— Isaiah 26:12

The connotation for the word "peace" can mean something different for different people. Is peace just a pop culture slogan of the 60s and 70s? I have found that when I apply biblical ideas to my own life, they make a whole lot more sense. Peace is more than just a word hippies tattooed on their forearms! Peace is having a calm heart in a chaotic world. Let God replace your anxieties with peace. According to Don Joseph Goewey, managing partner of ProAttitude, 85 percent of the things we worry about don't even happen. It will save you a lot of mental energy to trust in God. Decide in stressful moments today that you will rely on God's peace. It is His peace that should be at the center of your heart and mind.

PRAYER: Lord, I want to have Your peace when I'm feeling anxious or stressed out. Help me to trust You. Amen.

notes:

SWIMMING UPSTREAM

"But as for me, I watch in hope for the Lord, I wait for my God and Savior, my God will hear me."

— *Micah 7:7*

As Christians, sometimes we are like salmon in a mighty river, swimming upstream. People may question your motives and you may have to explain your faith. 1 Peter 3:15 says, "Always be prepared to give an answer to everyone who asks you to give the reason for the hope you profess." You can't hope in God without knowing Him. And you can't know Him without surrendering yourself. Notice that Micah's faith doesn't waver as he says the words in today's verse. He is completely certain that God will hear him. Micah declared that he was going to be faithful while he was waiting, and so can you! Let the things you do prove to those around you that your hope is instilled in Jesus Christ. It's not always easy, but it's always worth it.

PRAYER: Dear God, there is so much to hope for in You. I pray that I would take refuge in Your arms and not follow what others are doing around me. Thank You that You hear every one of my prayers and cries. Amen.

notes:

"You can't hope in God without knowing Him. And you can't know Him without surrendering yourself."

SEEING HIS GLORY

"Then Jesus said, 'Did I not tell you that if you believed, you would see the glory of God?'"

— *John 11:40*

Jesus said these words to Martha after her brother, Lazarus died. People were confused why Jesus didn't show up to prevent his death. If Mary and Martha hadn't experienced those four days of grief, Jesus would have never been able to create the miracle of Lazarus' resurrection! Everyone saw the glory of God! Yes, Jesus made Mary and Martha wait for the life of their brother, but He wasn't hard-hearted. Verse 35 in John chapter 11 says, "Jesus wept." This is a reminder that Jesus was fully human and fully God! He felt sympathy for what Mary and Martha were going through just as He feels sympathy for you. Maybe you are going through a Mary and Martha season, and everything seems dead. Remember that Jesus brings life and you will see His glory.

PRAYER: Jesus, help me to trust You when I don't understand why something is happening. I want to see Your glory. Amen.

notes:

DAY 108

ASK GOD TO MAKE YOU BRAVE

**"Be not afraid, O land; be glad and rejoice.
Surely the Lord has done great things."**

— Joel 2:21

Everyone has days where nothing seems to be going right. Maybe those days turn into weeks or months. The easiest thing to do in those situations is . . . complain. In fact, the world expects that out of you. They want to see you get angry. Sometimes I can tell that people are just waiting for me to crack under pressure. However, there is hope in the many blessings God has already given. Instead of being anxious, make an effort to be thankful. Instead of being afraid, ask the Lord to make you BRAVE! There is a saying that goes, "If He brings you to it, He'll bring you through it." Just think— God is sitting in heaven smiling at you because He's proud. He's proud of what you've accomplished in life and what you will accomplish. He's proud of you when you wake up and choose to live for Him another day, even on the tough days. Remember all the good things the Lord has done!

PRAYER: Father, let me remember the good things You have done when I am afraid or anxious. Thank You for caring for me. Amen.

**"Turn my eyes away from worthless things;
preserve my life according to Your word."**

— *Psalm* 119:37

When you think about our time on Earth compared to eternity, life is very short. As a little girl, my Grandma Kathy told me that I was going to be a grandma in the blink of an eye. I haven't exactly gotten to that point, but life sure does go by quickly! If life is like "a vapor"—here and gone so soon— doesn't that reinforce the fact that Christians should be completely devoted to God's Word? I constantly need to ask God to turn my eyes away from worthless things. When it comes down to it, the small things really don't matter. People got along fine without iPhones and computers and TVs in Jesus' day! Ask the Lord for focus as you live this short life, preparing for the eternal one!

PRAYER: Dear Jesus, please preserve my life and remind me that it's worthwhile. I pray that I would focus on Your truth instead of worthless things. Amen.

notes:

DAY
110

THE DISADVANTAGES OF TAKING ADVANTAGE

"Do not take advantage of each other, but fear your God. I am the Lord your God."

— *Leviticus* 25:7

If the truth hurts, this truth is as painful as stepping on a Lego in your bare feet: You can be selfish. But so can I. What do you do when you know you're wrapped around someone's finger or you have someone wrapped around your finger? I remember in elementary school asking a boy who liked me, to throw my trash away. Obviously that wasn't the nicest thing to do. Yet, that still happens in typical relationships today. One person could be madly in love, while the other person just wants to use them. This applies to any relationship, not just dating. Your younger siblings really look up to you (no matter how much they annoy you). Don't take advantage of them or be deceitful. Situations such as these allow God's people to humble themselves before Him and respect the people who care for them.

PRAYER: Dear God, open my eyes to see areas where I may have taken advantage of people. Let me put others first to further Your kingdom. Amen.

"Dear God, Open up my eyes to see areas where I may have taken advantage of people. Let me put others first to further Your kingdom."

"Children, obey your parents in the Lord, for this is right. 'Honor your father and mother'—which is the first commandment with a promise—that it may go well with you, and that you may enjoy a long life on the earth."

— Ephesians 6:1–3

I wouldn't be the person I am today without my parents (literally!). They have been the best godly examples in my life. I know that is not the case for everyone. Whether you're old or young, you've probably experienced some disagreements with your parents. Sometimes I can't get my own opinions out of my head! In those moments, I am humbled because my parents are usually right, and they know what's best for me. Are there moments when you have been bitter or unforgiving to your parents? I encourage you to restore any broken relationships, because time waits for no one—and regret can last a lifetime!

PRAYER: Dear Lord, forgive me for the times I have taken my parents for granted. Teach me to have patience and to honor my mom and dad so I can honor You. Amen.

notes:

FRIENDSHIP IS A GIFT

"Jonathan became one in the spirit with David, and he loved him as himself."

— I Samuel 18:1

The story of David and Jonathan makes me feel all happy inside. Friendship is a gift. In fact, the name "Jonathan" means, "God has given." God gave Jonathan the ability to be a caring friend. My brother, who happens to be named Jonathan, is a really good friend. He listens to everything I have to say and motivates me to believe in myself! He puts others before himself, and he's always open to how he can provide help. Maybe you have someone like Jonathan in your life. Maybe you could be that person to someone else. The love of God was meant to be shared and re-shared! People were made to care for one another. You never know what the person next to you is going through. Be their light, and be their Jonathan!

PRAYER: Dear Jesus, I want to be there for others, just like Jonathan was for David. Show me how to be a good friend. Amen.

notes:

SPIRIT, LEAD ME

"Trust in the Lord with all your heart and lean not on your own understanding; in all your ways acknowledge him, and he will make your paths straight."

— *Proverbs* 3:5–6

I have sung the song, "Oceans" by Hillsong more times than I could count. Each time, I poured my emotions into the lyrics that say, "Spirit, lead me where my trust is without borders." Then, I realized what it really means. To be honest, it made me feel uncomfortable. I was asking God to purposefully put me in places where my faith could be tested so I could trust Him more. Was that really my heart's desire? This verse reminds me that I don't even have to understand the tough parts of life to follow Jesus. Your path may be a little bumpy, but He will make your path straight. Life is so much more than praying for roses and daisies. Life is more like a rose bush; yes, it has its thorns, but with God's love poured out on us, the roses out-shine the thorns.

PRAYER: Lord, it's not always easy for me to accept the fact that I will be tested with hard times. Teach me how to trust You. Amen.

TAKE RISKS

**"Therefore keep watch, because you do not know
on what day your Lord will come."**

— *Matthew* 24:42

How do you feel when you think of the rapture and the return of Jesus? Do you feel like it's some crazy test you never studied for? All I know is that it would be one step closer to heaven. Quite often, I think about what I would do if I knew I only had one day to live. I think I would be fearless, not worrying about what other people thought of me. But isn't that how we're supposed to live every day anyway? The speaker at my brother's college graduation had his speech centered on two words: take risks [for God]. After all, 2 Timothy 1:7 says, "For God did not give us a spirit of timidity, but a spirit of power, of love and of self-discipline." Do something crazy for Jesus today, because life is short. He calls us to take risks!

PRAYER: Dear God, I pray that I treat every day as a new day to follow You—without fear. Life is a gift, and I want to use it to the fullest. Amen.

notes:

DAY
115

CALL AND HE WILL ANSWER

"Call to me and I will answer you and tell you great and unsearchable things you do not know."

— Jeremiah 33:3

Have you ever had one of those days when it seems like the end is never in sight? You're completely overwhelmed with what's in front of you. Maybe your emotions cause you to snap at people because you don't have all the answers. Guess what? Jesus has every single answer for everything. (Even the terrible chemistry questions.) Never doubt that God will bring you through your stress. This verse shares that He will tell you great and unsearchable things! Just call on Him when it feels like the ground is shifting from underneath you. James 1:5 reads, "If any of you lacks wisdom, he should ask God, who gives generously without finding fault . . . " You don't have to let the stressful moments cloud your faith.

PRAYER: Dear Lord, sometimes I need to be reminded that You have all the answers. Please give me Your wisdom in every aspect of my life. Amen.

notes:

DAY
116

MAKE HIM GREATER

"He must become greater; I must become less."

— John 3:30

Our society is being faced with the paradox of being too self-centered and too insecure. We worship other people's opinions while tearing other people down. There is no reward in that, only an endless cycle of emptiness. To "make God greater" is to look at the world from a different viewpoint. Many worries and anxieties are so small compared to what God has for us. If we realized that our job as Christians is simply to love people and not to please them, it could allow Him to become greater. Sometimes the Lord allows us to go through stressful situations so we can learn to trust Him. Remember that His strength is greater than yours. Look for opportunities in life to focus less on your fear, and search your daily life for His presence. God always knows what He's doing.

PRAYER: Dear God, please help me when I am thinking too much of my problems or myself. I want to make You greater in my life. Amen.

notes:

"Remember that His strength is greater than yours. Look for opportunities in life to focus less on your fear, and search your daily life for His presence."

DELIGHTFUL DESIRES

**"Delight yourself in the Lord and he will give
you the desires of your heart."**

— *Psalm 37:4*

You may have read this verse and thought, *What? God hasn't given me everything I wanted!* If we look at what David is saying from a worldly point of view, that's what it should mean. We put in our requests, and God pops out what we want . . . like a vending machine. However, the *Fire Bible* says, "God will answer the deepest cries of our hearts if our desires are in line with His desires and purposes." God knows every little feeling you express and every feeling you keep bottled up inside. He sees your heartbreak. He sees your goals and ambitions. He sees you when you have to make tough decisions. Before seeking for joy in yourself, delight in the Lord. Let His joy become your joy!

PRAYER: Dear Jesus, thank You that You see my heart. In moments when I am worried, please remind me that You know everything, and You only do good things. Amen.

notes:

DAY 118

JONAH AND EVERY
DISTANCE RUNNER

"The word of the Lord came to Jonah, son of Amittai: 'Go to the great city of Nineveh and preach against it, because its wickedness has come up before me.' But Jonah ran away from the Lord and headed for Tarshish."

— *Jonah 1:1–3a*

If you have grown up going to church, you've probably heard many VBS (Vacation Bible School) stories, Sunday school lessons, or crazy songs about Jonah. Sometimes repetitiveness can take away effectiveness. But when you think about it, we are all like Jonah. Even with simple tasks in daily life, we procrastinate and try to avoid them. You can ask anyone in my family, and they would tell you that I am not a morning person. This doesn't help me when I am supposed to run seven or eight miles after I wake up. The longer I wait to run, the hungrier I get. I waste more time, and it goes further into the heat of the day (not ideal for a distance runner in the summer). As I have experienced running away from my running, I imagine Jonah felt similarly. By procrastinating, he was making it harder for himself, and he was pushing away what God had for him.

PRAYER: Dear Lord, I pray that I wouldn't hesitate when You call me to do something. Let me be willing to wake up and conquer each task for You. Amen.

I'LL BELIEVE IT WHEN I SEE IT

"Then he said to Thomas, 'Put your finger here; see my hands. Reach out your hand and put it into my side. Stop doubting and believe.'"

— John 20:27

What can unfulfilled promises, low expectations, and preconceived ideas lead to? Doubt. Doubt seems to come after us like little kids running for the ice cream truck (even though I will gladly run for the ice cream truck until I'm too old to run at all!). Doubt can get us down in the dumps with a "Woe is me" attitude. It's socially acceptable. However, my dad once said that if you're sad, don't stay there. Move on. Extended sadness can lead to doubt, and doubt is the opposite of hope. The nickname "Doubting Thomas" was actually named after this Thomas from the Bible. Anyone could point out his flaws for not having hope in Jesus, but we've all been there. Don't allow the doubts from the devil to replace the hope from Jesus in your life.

PRAYER: Dear God, please forgive me for all the times I have doubted You or Your power. Help me to stop doubting and believe. Amen.

HATERS GONNA HATE

"Do not set foot on the path of the wicked or walk in the way of evil men . . . for they cannot sleep till they do evil. They are robbed of slumber till they make someone fall."

— *Proverbs* 4:14, 16

Sometimes people can be jerks. There's no way around it. You will never make it through life (much less a day) without someone being rude to you. But, in the words of Taylor Swift, "Haters gonna hate!" So why am I bringing this verse to your attention? If I expect life to be entirely wonderful, it's not preparing me to be firm in my faith. I am so thankful that Jesus never gave up on you or me because of the persecution He went through. Imagine all He suffered; He was still willing to save the world. The next time somebody rubs you the wrong way, do not stoop down to his or her level of negativity. Christians should be the happiest people on the planet, not because we live perfectly joyful lives, but because we have a perfectly joyful God.

PRAYER: Jesus, thank You for dealing with difficult people so You could save me. Nothing I will face could ever compare to what You went through. Help me to focus on You instead of what others say or do. Amen.

"I am so thankful that Jesus never gave up on you or me because of the persecution He went through. Imagine all He suffered; He was still willing to save the world."

WE ALL NEED CORRECTION

"Preach the word; be prepared in season and out of season; correct, rebuke and encourage—with great patience and careful instruction."

— 2 Timothy 4:2

The last part of this verse is what really sticks out to me the most . . . "With great patience and careful instruction." Correcting someone does not have to involve rudeness. You can be an example for others without degrading them or trying to belittle them. The fact is, we all need to be corrected sometimes. Sure, it can be embarrassing when my friends or family bring up something I don't want to hear. But what if God is using them as a vessel to reach my selfish heart? Allow yourself to be held accountable, and also be prepared to pull out the patient love of God from your pocket whenever it's needed.

PRAYER: Dear Father, remind me that Your love has no boundaries. Help me to love others when they need Your truth, and soften my heart when I need it. Amen.

notes:

BELIEVE IN GOD'S DREAMS FOR YOU

"Do not be afraid or discouraged because of this vast army. For the battle is not yours, but God's."

— 2 Chronicles 20:15b

During my junior year of high school, I had a really special track team. There was something about everyone putting in effort for a common cause. My sophomore year, we ended up finishing eighth place in the state. On the bus ride home, my coach said, "We're gonna win this next year." I thought to myself, "Yeah, right!" One year later, we were State Champions at the MITCA (Michigan Interscholastic Track Coaches Association) Division III Team State Meet. I'm not saying this to say that sports are all about winning. Instead, I would like to point out what we had to overcome. I ran the four longest races in track: the 4x8 relay, the 800 Meter run, the 1600 Meter (1 Mile), and the 3200 Meter (2 Mile). Running is very physical, but it's extremely hard mentally as well. When we all heard that we won first in the state, my coach (Coach K) shouted at us, "The next time someone tells you dreams can't come true, look them in the eye and say, 'Yes they do!'" I think this can relate to our Christian faith. The next time God calls you to do something outside of your comfort zone, believe in His dreams for you!

PRAYER: Dear Jesus, sometimes it is hard to believe that I am capable of all you have called me to do. Allow my heart to dream big dreams for Your Kingdom. Amen.

notes:

FADS AND FANCIES WILL NOT CARRY OUR FUTURE

"Neither their silver nor their gold will be able to save them on the day of the Lord's wrath."

— Zephaniah 1:18

As the world becomes filled with more and more "stuff," our time on Earth becomes shorter and shorter. No one will be able to take his or her 14-carat-gold wedding ring or fancy car to heaven. This verse is a reminder that anything we are able to buy or possess is so much smaller than what God has in store for our future. Isn't it crazy to think that we'll be with Jesus forever? There will literally be no ends or boundaries. I find myself worrying too often about which shoes are in style and whether I should eat ice cream for the fifth day in a row! Sorry to break it to you, but we won't be able to bribe our way into heaven with ice cream or Hunter boots.

PRAYER: Dear God, please help me to focus more on You instead of fads, foods, or fancy things. I don't want to make excuses for my life when I face You. Amen.

notes:

"All men will hate you because of me, but he who stands firm to the end will be saved."

— *Mark* 13:13

If you think about it, living as a Christian is kind of like being in the Hunger Games. (Work with me here.) Your life is broadcasted for everyone to see. There will always be people who attack you with harsh words and different opinions. And, like the verse says above, you have to be strong to make it to the end. Saying, "All men will hate you" is a bit harsh, but let's think of the alternative. I would not want the world to fall in love with me for calling myself a follower of Christ; I'd want them to fall in love with Jesus! The Christian life is never about drawing attention to ourselves. Once we realize that, it makes it easier to accept the fact that we weren't made to please ourselves or others—just God. Even if your peers give you a hard time, remember to stand firm.

PRAYER: Lord, following You is not easy when the world has so much criticism. I want to be strong throughout this race of life. Amen.

notes:

STAY HUMBLE AND STAY CLOSE

"God opposes the proud but gives grace to the humble. Submit yourselves, then, to God. Resist the devil, and he will flee from you."

— James 4:6b–7

When I think of the word, "submit," I think of submitting answers for a digital test. If you're anything like me, you may put a lot of pressure on yourself to do well. When I have pressed that "submit" button after an important and stressful test, I find myself experiencing so much relief and peace. That's what it should be like when you submit yourself to God. (It's an even better relief than finally finishing the SAT!) If you humble yourself, realizing we all need a Savior, God will honor that. The more you submit to God, the more the devil will try to attack you. Why? Because he's scared of what God can do through you! So, stay humble and stay close to God. The enemy doesn't stand a chance because the battle has already been won.

PRAYER: Dear Lord, please help me to remember that it's not only okay to surrender to You, but it's what best for me. I can't do it on my own. Amen.

DAY 126

ALL THINGS NEW

**"He who was seated on the throne said,
'I am making all things new.'"**

— *Revelation 20:5a*

It's so amazing that God cares about our hearts. He's more than just the "Guy in the sky" or the "Man upstairs." In order to make "all things new," it means God has been where you have been. You can't make something new if you don't have a frame of reference for how it was before. He sees when your days start to feel longer and harder. But don't give up! This verse says that God is on the throne! There can't be two rulers of your heart. If He knows everything, why should we even try to tell God what He can and cannot do? If you are in a drought season, where God seems distant, be expectant of His power because He makes the old brand new. 2 Corinthians 5:17 reminds us, "The old has gone. The new is here!"

PRAYER: Father, I thank You that You see where I have been in my life. You know how to make the bad become good and the old become new. Amen.

notes:

"If you are in a drought season, where God seems distant, be expectant of His power because He makes the old brand new. 2 Corinthians 5:17 reminds us, 'The old has gone. The new is here.'"

BUILDING THE KINGDOM

**"For he is the living God and he endures forever;
his Kingdom will not be destroyed,
his dominion will never end."**

— *Daniel 6:26b*

The fact that God's kingdom will never be destroyed means Christians should do everything they can to build the kingdom up. Will it be scary to talk to your peers about God? Yes. But it will be worth it to say you've tried when the end times come and people's earthly and eternal lives are on the line. And if God is living as Scripture says, He is constantly doing work in you! That means you can have a conversation with Him. That means He could never die or give up on you. There is literally nothing ever created that could separate you from the love of Jesus Christ.

PRAYER: Dear God, I'm so thankful for Your protection over my life. I want to remember that You're constantly sitting on Your throne. Help me to share Your saving grace with others. Amen.

notes:

A FATHER FOR EVERYONE

"How great is the love the Father has lavished on us, that we should be called children of God!"

— 1 John 3:1

Being a child of God means that you are literally fully loved by Him. We are all children of God. Verses in the Bible are just words on a page until you make a personal connection. Whenever I would hear that I was a child of God as a kid, I didn't really think anything of it. I didn't grow up in a broken home. I have always had my parents' support. But I was looking at everything from the wrong perspective. If you have grown up without stable parents, God is the loving Father you never had. If you have grown up with a good childhood and present parents, God is so much more loving than your earthly father ever could be. No matter what your past is, God is meant to be a Father for everyone.

PRAYER: Dear God, let me remember how special it is to be Your child. Thank You for choosing me. Amen.

notes:

SWEET TOOTH JAZZY

"Is not God in the heights of heaven? And see how lofty are the highest stars! Yet you say, 'What does God know?'"

— *Job 22:12–13a*

To say I had a sweet tooth as a child would be an understatement. My mom tells me this story of when she had to stand on stage on a Sunday morning and announce to my church, "Please don't give Jasmine any more candy." Apparently, I would go up to any woman with a purse and ask for chocolate, mints, or gum. (I resist the temptation to do that now.) I'm sure I was disappointed the next time I asked for candy but didn't receive any. But my mom knew what she was doing, because my seven cavities came back to haunt me! Basically, there are times in life when we want to have fun, and we think we know better than anyone else. We push God aside while we cram our souls with things of low substance. So put down the tempting "candy," because God is sparing you from the cavities!

PRAYER: Dear Lord, there are times when I feel like I know better than You. Please remind me that if You made the stars, You know how to direct my life, too. Amen.

A LITTLE FAITH GOES A LONG WAY

**"If you falter in times of trouble,
how small is your strength!"**

— Proverbs 24:10

My brother Jonathan always says you know you're going toward the will of God when the enemy starts firing at you. But what should you do when something knocks you down? Get back up. It's so true that people's true colors show when things are going wrong. I don't consider myself an angry person, but there are times in life when I simply want to stop trying. If the devil represents life's "haters," you've got to stand on the strength of God and prove those haters wrong. The Bible says in Matthew 17 that with faith just the size of a mustard seed, powerful things can happen through God. Don't be a wavering follower of Christ, swayed by minor distractions. Rise above your time of trouble to fight back against the enemy.

PRAYER: Jesus, I don't want to be known as a person with small strength. I pray that You would help me to rely on You and Your infinite strength. Amen.

notes:

"Don't be a wavering follower of Christ, swayed by minor distractions. Rise above your time of trouble to fight back against the enemy."

MAKE CHURCH MORE THAN GOING THROUGH THE MOTIONS

"My people come to you, as they usually do, and sit before you to listen to your words, but they do not put them into practice. With their mouths they express devotion, but their hearts are greedy for unjust gain."

— Ezekiel 33:31

These words spoken by Ezekiel to God fully explain the term, "going through the motions." This is what my typical Sunday looks like: Wake up around 6:30 a.m. to be at church for worship practice by 7:30 a.m. Go to Sunday school at 9:00 a.m. Play piano and sing for the adult church service at 10:00 a.m. Find time in my day to run. Print off music sheets and chords for youth group songs. Get to church by 5:00 p.m. for another worship practice, and finally go to youth group from 6–8 p.m. I'm exhausted just by writing all of that! My point is this—I have filled my time with so much ministry that I need to make sure my heart is still in the right place. Whether you rarely go to church or you basically live there, we should never treat church as one more thing to check off our lists.

PRAYER: Father, forgive me for all the times I was just going through the motions. Church should always be about me focusing on more of You. Amen.

HOSEA'S WIFE

"The Lord said to me, 'Go, show your love to your wife again, though she is loved by another and is an adulteress. Love her as the Lord loves the Israelites, though they turn to other gods . . .'"

— *Hosea 3:1*

When I hear of spouses cheating on each other, it makes me sadder than anything. In our culture, it's completely acceptable to leave someone after he or she is unfaithful. But could you imagine God calling a man to stay with his wife even after she betrayed him? Isn't that unsettling? Someone who invested so much time and effort into a relationship deserves better. Truth is . . . we are all like Hosea's wife. We search for love in other places instead of turning to God first. He has poured care and attention into His children, yet we still think it's not enough. In the next verse of Hosea Chapter 3, Hosea goes back to claim what was rightfully God's, and He will always go back for you.

PRAYER: Dear God, I'm so sorry for all the times I haven't been faithful to You. Thank You for showing me that my true value is in You. Amen.

SEEK THE LORD

"'For I know the plans I have for you,' declares the Lord, 'plans to prosper you and not to harm you, plans to give you hope and a future. Then you will call upon me and come and pray to me, and I will listen to you. You will seek me and find me when you seek me with all your heart.'"

— *Jeremiah* 29:11–13

The Scripture verse Jeremiah 29:11 is kind of like the *Frozen* of all Disney movies! Yes, it is quoted very often, but don't ignore the Lord's original intention with this verse. It is a wonderful depiction of the relationship between man and God. God recognizes that we need Him to plan our lives, and we should choose Him as our source of comfort. I think it is interesting how these three verses tie together. Sure, God wants to give us a positive future, but he also expects us to seek Him. What is "seeking God?" It is recognizing all the ways you can follow Him better. Verse 13 says that you will seek God when you seek Him with all your heart. I encourage you to not just say that God is the most important thing in your life, but to literally lift Him up and seek Him in all aspects of your life.

PRAYER: Dear Lord, as I trust in Your plans for me, help me to presently seek You and Your heart. I want others to see that I am actively following You each and every day. Amen.

SHOW GOD'S GOODNESS

"Be very careful, then, how you live—not as unwise, but as wise, making the most of every opportunity, because the days are evil."

— *Ephesians* 5:15–16

I apologize for being a Debby Downer, but our days on Earth probably won't become simpler. Terrorist attacks, mass shootings, and natural disasters seem to be increasingly in the news. All of this to say: Respect the value of life (yours and everyone else's). It may be cheesy, but each moment really is a gift. Paul is telling us in this verse to make the most of every opportunity. Hold the door for people. Call up your amazing grandparents. Write a friend or coworker a nice letter. Be smart, and don't worry about little things. There is so much bad in the world that someone needs to step in the world and show God's goodness.

PRAYER: Dear Father, I never want to be scared of what's happening in the world. Help me to remember that I am living this life for a reason. Amen.

notes:

BE JOYFUL, PRAY, AND GIVE THANKS

"Be joyful always; pray continually; give thanks in all circumstances, for this is God's will for you in Christ Jesus."

— 1 Thessalonians 5:16–18

I believe that this verse shows three things everyone struggles with. When I am running late in the morning, and I am feeling stressed, I don't want to be joyful about the situation. I don't want to give thanks. When I am preoccupied and I fill my time with other things, my prayer life is not consistent. When I'm experiencing an injury at the worst time possible, it's not always first on my radar to give thanks. Yet, all of those little struggles are why I need a lot more of Jesus. Growing deeper in God means training yourself to stop and hear His voice. The entertaining YouTube video you are about to watch will still be there tomorrow. The thing you're stressed about today, you may not remember a year from now. Make the choice to better your thinking with the kingdom of God.

PRAYER: Dear Lord, please help me when I get impatient or distracted. I want to try harder to have a joyful attitude, no matter my circumstances, and to pray more. Amen.

notes:

BE JOYFUL LIKE A CHILD

"Anyone who does not receive the kingdom of God like a little child will never enter it."

— *Luke* 18:17

Kids make me so happy. I unleash all my goofiness when I'm with them! In March of 2017, I competed in Michigan's District Fine Arts Festival in the category of Children's Lesson Solo. I didn't know what to expect since I had never done that category before, but through God's help I actually received the merit award (first in the state)! What I like so much about kids is that they have an abundance of joy pent up inside of them. Sure, there's a meltdown in the supermarket every once in a while, but there's nothing like the giggle of a toddler. Jesus was calling His disciples and followers in the Bible to be like children because He wanted them to experience that same joy and fascination of Him. Children also are fully dependent on their parents, just as we should be with God. There is no one else who deserves our attention more than Him. In addition to being dependent on God and having joy in Him, He also calls us to have an unwavering childlike faith.

PRAYER: Dear Jesus, please teach me to have the same joy and faith that a child has. I want to humble myself before you to fully experience Your glory. Amen.

"What I like so much about kids is that they have an abundance of joy pent up inside of them. Sure, there's a meltdown in the supermarket every once in a while, but there's nothing like the giggle of a toddler."

NO FEAR IN LOVE

"There is no fear in love. But perfect love drives out fear."

— 1 John 4:18

Nothing of this world can truly be declared as "perfect." The newest iPhone or Samsung models can still break down. If you're like me, your socks still have holes in them. The strongest structure of wood can still be burned to the ground. People have off days and say harsh things. But the love of God will never fail. It can't be broken. It can't be torn like a piece of paper. The love of God does not need a computer program to prevent minimal human errors. The Lord existed before anything else. Think of all the things—the man-made things—you place your trust in every single day. You trust that your car will stop when you hit the brake pedal. You trust your GPS to bring you to your destination. How much more can we trust our perfect God who is above it all?

PRAYER: Dear Lord, I want to fully trust in Your unfailing love. Help me to realize You know and see every aspect of my life through the eyes of love. Amen.

notes:

DAY
138

THE LORD CAN RAISE YOU UP

**"And the prayer offered in faith will make the sick person
well; the Lord will raise him up. If he has sinned,
he will be forgiven."**

— *James* 5:15

Prayers don't get lost in the mail. Prayers aren't texts that God just forgot to respond to. Prayers are long term! One prayer you say now can affect people centuries down the road. I have learned that sickness humbles people to be more vulnerable than they ever have been. If I had a dollar for every time I cried to God because of various foot problems, I could probably buy myself a new foot! The point is, those moments were all times when I cried to Jesus with a deeper passion than I had before. Even though I have dealt with dozens of foot wraps, ankle tapes, boots, and moments on crutches, I am still alive and well! Just like this verse says—the Lord raised me up, and He has the power to do the same for you! Never give up on your prayers.

PRAYER: God, I never like being sick, injured, or ill or if someone I know is. In those moments, help me to pray harder and believe more than I ever have before. Amen.

HIS MERCIES ARE NEW EVERY MORNING

"The Lord is slow to anger and great in power; the Lord will not leave the guilty unpunished . . . "

— Nahum 1:3a

Imagine if one person was given all the power God has. He or she would probably tend to get greedy and show anger and hostility. I don't know about you, but I do not like being in situations where people feel angry. I'm usually a pretty positive person, so anger tends to make me feel uncomfortable. You would normally think that punishing people and being patient would both be contradictory. Not for God. He is the perfect blend of love and direction. Only He is capable of seeing seven billion people's faults and being slow to anger. Many people think God is like the hammer in the game of whack-a-mole, getting ready to punish anyone who pops up. The Bible says that His mercies are new every morning. God is just, but He will never stop being merciful.

PRAYER: Dear Lord, thank You for being patient with me and forgiving me. I love You. Amen.

notes:

KEEP YOUR MORALS HIGH

"If she is a wall, we will build towers of silver on her. If she is a door, we will enclose her with panels of cedar."

— *Song of Songs 8:9*

This verse is a reminder that everyone will face temptation sometime in life, whether they are "baby Christians" or they have been Christians for many years. It's important for young teenagers to realize this temptation, so they have a plan of action for when it comes! In verse nine, I like to think of the "wall" as the woman's morals. If her morals are strong and she resists inappropriate sexual urges, she will be honored. If she is willing to fall for any guy who gives her attention (a door), her heart will need to be protected. When temptations or problems with relationships arise, remember to keep your chin high and your morals higher.

PRAYER: Dear God, forgive me for the times I have given in to any temptation in my relationships. I want my beliefs and my actions to firmly reflect You. Amen.

notes:

"When temptations or problems
with relationships arise,
remember to keep your chin high
and your morals higher."

DAY 141

GOD WORKS WONDERS

**"You will have plenty to eat, until you are full,
and you will praise the name of the Lord your God,
who has worked wonders for you;
never again will my people be shamed."**

— *Joel 2:26*

What do you cling to in times of trouble? Do you "pig out" on ice cream and binge on watching old TV shows on Netflix? Do you find comfort in confiding with friends and family? I'd be lying if I said that I'm not tempted to do the first one! But for me, I find my confidence in life knowing that I have hope in Jesus. Before verse 26 in this chapter of Joel, it's described that many people's crops were destroyed—their way of making a living and receiving food was demolished. If you translate this story to modern day, maybe someone gets laid off his or her job and he or she doesn't know what to do with his or her life. But God promised the people in Joel's day that He would be faithful in difficult times, and that still applies to present times. There is no One better to put your hope in than Jesus Christ.

PRAYER: Dear Jesus, sometimes it's hard for me to have faith when it seems like my whole world has shifted. Let me be re-minded of Your hope. Thank You for working wonders for all Your people. Amen.

HIS PROMISES LAST FOREVER

"My name will be great among the nations, from the rising to the setting of the sun."

— *Malachi 1:11a*

Think about just how vast the world we live in is. There are so many cultures and countries that I will never experience. Who else could create complex mountain ranges and powerful waterfalls but God? All of this emphasizes the greatness of our Lord. He loves you as much as He loves the biggest celebrity, the humblest pastor, the smallest child, or even the worst sinner. We are all people experiencing the gift of life. When Jesus comes back, everyone on the Earth will see Him. Every single person. That is literally incomprehensible. Every human will see Him for who He really is, just as Jesus has seen who His people are (on Earth and in heaven). The next time you hear about some bizarre place in the world, remember that the God who created that "bizarre place" wants to have a personal relationship with you, and His promises last forever.

PRAYER: Dear Lord, thank You for creating the Earth and all of the nations in it. Help me to be globally aware, remembering how vast Your love is for every single person. Amen.

THE FIRST SHALL BE LAST

"He has brought down rulers from their thrones but has lifted up the humble."

— *Luke* 1:52

Do the right thing, even when no one is watching. As many times as you have heard that saying, its value still holds true. God does not look at His children based on their status or fame. In fact, He blesses the servants in the world—the people who don't seek recognition. Matthew 20:16 says, "So the last will be first, and the first will be last." Just because someone has fame and glory here on Earth, it does not solidify him or her a spot in heaven. When people are complimenting you left and right, stay humble. When things don't go your way and you're at the bottom, stay humble, not bitter. You never know what each day will bring. The moment you decide you like the taste of success better than the taste of His Word, remember that all good things start with Him.

PRAYER: Dear God, help me to not get a big head with things I am good at. You deserve all the glory in this life. I want to be humble for You no matter my circumstances. Amen.

notes:

LET GOD RENEW YOU TODAY

"Restore us to yourself, O Lord, that we may return; renew our days as of old."

— *Lamentations* 5:21

No matter what happens on Earth, it doesn't affect the goodness in heaven. When we feel like we are far away from the Lord, it's never Him who pulls away from us. If you asked God to restore yourself back to when you had a strong relationship with Him, that is still not reaching His potential. This verse is a plea to be restored back to God himself. All of our blessings are picked out and planned out by God, and we should use them to bring honor to Him. In my past experiences, the first step in restoration is allowing yourself to receive it by breaking down any pride. God's best for you will always be more important than being a part of the "in" crowd. Let God renew you today. Don't wait until you get to church. Don't wait until you hear a sermon. Don't wait for a worship service at a huge conference or rally. Don't wait for Christmas or Easter. God wants to take you where you are now and make you brand new.

PRAYER: Dear Lord, I apologize for all the times my pride has gotten in the way of being renewed by You. Help me to become more active in my faith than I've ever been before. Amen.

NOTHING IS IMPOSSIBLE WITH GOD

"I was personally unknown to the churches of Judea that are in Christ. They only heard the report: 'The man who formerly persecuted us is now preaching the faith he once tried to destroy. And they praised God because of me.'"

— *Galatians 2:22–24*

This passage of Scripture was written by Paul, who formerly condemned Christians. Could you imagine disagreeing entirely with a person and then having him teach you his new beliefs? My natural instinct would probably be judgment. How can this person bash us and then try to become one of us? That is so hypocritical. But, that's not what the people in the churches said. They praised and thanked God for Paul's transformation. Even if we are not outwardly showing negativity like Paul, we are all in desperate need of the Lord's grace. Strive to be someone that others praise God for. Lastly, never minimize what the Lord can do. If there are people in your life who don't know God, keep praying for them. They may just have a Paul moment. Nothing is impossible with God.

PRAYER: Dear God, I pray that You would teach me how to ask for forgiveness and how to accept other people. Help me to not give up on people who are lost. I love You. Amen.

DAY
146

BUILD YOUR HOUSE
WITH THE BLUEPRINT

**"Consequently faith comes from hearing the message,
and the message is heard through the Word of Christ."**

— *Romans 10:17*

How can you believe something if you don't know what you are believing? There are so many opinions in our society regarding politics and social issues. Sometimes, I have to tell myself that I don't know what I believe if I haven't fully looked into a topic. This doesn't have to be the case with our relationship with Jesus! To believe is to know, and to know is to be willing to learn. The Word of God has an abundance of truth with answers flowing out of it. Before you claim to be a follower of Christ, look deeper into what it entails. A friend of mine once said that being a Christian without reading the Bible is like building a house without the blueprint. The more you read His Word, the stronger your faith will be.

PRAYER: Dear Lord, I want to base my relationship with You off of Your Word. Thank You for giving me a source of constant comfort and contact. Amen.

notes:

"A friend of mine once said that being a Christian without reading the Bible is like building a house without the blueprint. The more you read His Word, the stronger your faith will be."

DAY 147

SIMPLY BE KIND

"And be ye kind to one another, tenderhearted, forgiving one another, even as God for Christ's sake has forgiven you."

— *Ephesians 4:32*

Those who have sat at my high school lunch table could testify to the fact that I have the tendency to be sassy. As a kid, I was classified as a "know-it-all," and when I strongly disagree with someone, I feel the childhood Jasmine arising! But God calls us to lay down our pride. He wants us to experience His grace. He wants us to simply be kind to other people. We think of random acts of kindness as speaking out praises, but kindness can also be using self-control and forgiveness to keep our mouths shut! God will give us the wisdom for when to speak and when to listen. Because when it comes down to it, we are all in need of God's forgiveness. Everyone is the same amount of worthy—unworthy! We don't need money or talent to be kind. We just need to open our eyes!

PRAYER: Dear Jesus, thanks for dealing with me and keeping me around, even though I don't deserve it. I want to have self-control and forgive others. Thank You for showing me what forgiveness really is. Amen.

DAY 148

LET HIS PEACE GUIDE YOU

"Whether you turn to the right or to the left, your ears will hear a voice behind you, saying, 'This is the way; walk in it!'"

— Isaiah 30:21

Decisions are hard. I'm probably one of the most indecisive people (besides my sister, Victoria. Love ya!). All types of people struggle with where they want to go to school and what they want to do with their lives. For me, both of those decisions were shockingly easy. Surprise! Crazy, right? Since sixth grade, I've never had any second thoughts about being an elementary school teacher. Spring Arbor University was the only college I applied to, and the only one I seriously considered. I know that the words "easy" and "decision" are rarely in the same sentence together. This verse is so comforting because God is basically saying, "No matter what choices you make—good ones or bad—I'll always be right there." Sometimes it can be a little scary when you feel like God isn't speaking right in front of you. Maybe it's because He's giving you directions from behind. Whether your choices are as easy as pie or they are very challenging, have peace through Jesus and walk in His way.

PRAYER: Dear Lord, please guide me in all directions of my life. Let me always be near to You and Your heart. Amen.

DAY 149

"Giving thanks always for all things unto God and the Father in the name of our Lord Jesus Christ."

— *Ephesians* 5:20

Think about the last time you were really annoyed. Maybe someone said something that wasn't kind. Maybe you embarrassed yourself in front of a lot of people (the story of my life). However, even on our worst days, there is still something to be thankful for. One day I was upset with the fact that my parents wouldn't let me do something. So, I started to cry in my car in the parking lot of a grocery store. It's lame, but we are all human. Honestly, what I was crying about was something that I could have gotten over in less than a minute. Looking back, I could have been thanking God for the car I was in, parents who care about me, and money to buy groceries. Ephesians 5:20 reminds us to give thanks to the Lord always, even when we don't get our way. If you are able to read this book right now, you are considered a privileged person. Never forget the simple joys of life, and give thanks.

PRAYER: God, I am sorry for the times I have let my attitude come in the way of showing my thanks toward You. Please teach me how to be more grateful. Amen.

SHOW MERCY ABOVE ALL

"Be merciful, just as your Father is merciful."

— *Luke* 6:36

I need this reminder every day of my life. It is so easy to jump to conclusions: This person didn't show up to this because he or she didn't care about it, because he or she was hanging out with the crowd, because he or she is just like them. I need to stop trying to figure everyone else out so I can figure out more of who Jesus is. Who am I to put people in their places? A song called, "Mercy" by Bethel Music states, "You delight in showing mercy. And mercy triumphs over judgment." So, if the God of the universe can look past the dirt and flaws, shouldn't we all also extend graciousness to those around us? Here's the point: it is impossible to know all the challenges other people face. All experiences—the good, the bad, and the ugly—are what make humans humans. Followers of Christ should be overjoyed to show mercy on a daily basis.

PRAYER: Dear Lord, please forgive me for the times I have judged others. Let me see them through Your eyes so I can be gracious and merciful. Amen.

notes:

"So, if the God of the universe can look past the dirt and the flaws, shouldn't we all also extend graciousness to those around us? Followers of Christ should be overjoyed to show mercy on a daily basis."

A SPOKEN WORD
BY JASMINE HARPER

"Be the Church"

When did the church stop being about people?
"How are you?" "I'm good" is the extent of conversations
under the steeple.
How are you is just a pass to quickly get through
the *gate* of the congregation.
I'm good is a renewal to the ticket of your safe haven.
Don't get me wrong, there's nothing wrong with small talk . . .
It's just that talking small puts up a wall between you and His call.

When did the church stop being still in His presence?
We're perfectly programmed to perform pretense.
We can't delight in His light without lights of our own.
We can only hear His voice so astounding when our
sound is resounding.

Matthew 18:20 says the church is where two or more are gathered,
Rather than just a building used to sit on pews.
Acts 2:42 says to be devoted to the apostles' teaching
We can't exclude the truth—we can't pick and choose.

Hear me out. I'm not bashing church, quite the opposite.
Through church I found faith. I found hope, and that's positive.

Instead, I'm calling all leaders, all teachers, all breathers, all believers
To see beyond the pattern of church and become truth-seekers

Because the Holy Spirit does not fit in a box
He is wild and free
He can't be tamed with the same remote control
Used for your TV.

The Holy Spirit does not fit in a box
With only suits and ties and dresses
He takes you as you are
He wants all of you and your messes.

The Holy Spirit does not fit in a box
When you're hanging with your church friends
He wants to be shared with everyone you know
In every way your time is spent.

The Holy Spirit does not fit in a box
Of Sunday mornings or Wednesday nights
He wants to transform not just those days,
But your entire life.

The Holy Spirit does not fit in a box
In a time frame of 10:00 a.m. to noons
He's ready for you to encounter him at any moment
An encounter that outlasts the honeymoon.

We cannot be so busy with church that we don't
love people *in* the church.
We cannot be so busy with church that we don't
love people *outside* the church.

Revival is defined as an improvement in the condition or
strength of something.
Let us come together as the church and lift up the hope that
Christ brings.

Because the Holy Spirit does not fit in a box
And neither does a revival.
Be God's holy church. Get out of your comfort zones
Before the Lord's arrival.

"Who is this baby?"

She thinks about the nights she cried
When the tears were as abundant as blue seaside
With the world telling her that her thighs are too wide,
She doesn't know that she's beautiful inside

Because of her hair that's fried and the tears she hides,
She has much less than an ounce of pride
Let me just say that society has lied
Because beauty comes when confidence is applied
And insecurity has died

But she doesn't know that, she doesn't understand
She concludes her confidence comes from a man
Looking at her reflection,
The only thing in her head is the devil's deception

The next day, there's a guy—he's calling her name
"How 'bout we hang out after the game?"

She doesn't know what to think,
She tries not to blink
Her sadness, it sinks
It sinks
He picks up some drinks

A month later, the guy is gone
The memories and things they did—they continue to live on

Her parents assert,
"Oh, Doctor,
Would you spare her?
She's a teenager,
Not ready to be a mother
It's not worth it to deliver
We'll pay you to have it over
This is something we can't cover."

There's a young voice as quiet as a mouse
That still shouts
Mommy, Mommy!
I love you.
Mommy, mommy!
Do you love me?

The life inside her
Would change her world forever
A life to save or a life to lose
Chasing her choices, she still must choose

But then she realizes the significance
And the innocence
Of this infant.
She decides this baby's important

"I'm going to make myself better,"
Says that strong go-getter
She starts to pray,

Knowing that her value is not in that bae
But through the Way

The child, it arrives
With massive blue eyes
She says, "Thank God you're alive.
He saved us that night
I almost said goodbye."

Who is this baby?
This baby is you.
This baby is me.
Rescued by a man who died on a tree
We could have died, laying in the grave
Surrounded by sin, forced to be its slave

You see, that is not the case.
My father . . . erased the trace of disgrace.
It was replaced with His embrace.

And when you say,
"Daddy, Daddy.
Do you love me?
From this Daddy, Daddy
He says, "Unconditionally."

A SONGWRITING SELECTION
BY JASMINE HARPER

"Valleys"

Verse 1:
There is a joy greater than anything the world gives
There is a hope purer than riches, gold, or diamonds
There is a peace better than all my understanding
Through these trials, I'll hold on to what I know Your plan is

Chorus
(God I need You to) fill my valleys
Lower my mountains
My heart is hollow
But Your love's a fountain

Verse 2:
There is a love sweeter than anything I've tasted
There is a voice truer than every word that's been said
There is a pow'r stronger than walls that I've been trapped in
Through the storm, I'll have faith, 'cause You make life worth living

(Chorus)
(God I need You to) fill my valleys
Lower my mountains
My heart is hollow
But Your love's a fountain

Bridge:
Let Your beauty compel me
To see things the way You see
Let Your presence overwhelm me
And bring me down to my knees

(Chorus)
(God I need You to) fill my valleys
Lower my mountains
My heart is hollow
But Your love's a fountain

ACKNOWLEDGMENTS

Dan Van Veen – You edited the great majority of this book and helped me to articulate my thoughts clearly. Thank you for the countless hours and insights along the way!

Maryanna Young – You have helped two Harpers publish books by now! Thank you for guiding me in this process and helping me go from my "blank" to my book!

Lauren Manderbach and Alloy Signature – You have such a talented eye for photography and design. Thank you for capturing my heart through your lens.

Mrs. Bonnie Rae Walter and Fellowship of Christian Athletes (FCA) – Thank you so much for your encouragement on those early Friday mornings. You always know what is going on in students' lives, and you are one of the best prayer warriors I know! I'm proud to have been a part of the oldest Fellowship of Christian Athletes Huddle in the state of Michigan!

Coach Kyle McKown – Where do I begin? Thanks for being my favorite middle school teacher and the best coach I could have asked for. You have always brought the perfect balance of goofiness and seriousness. I would have not completed any of my goals in running without you. I will forever cherish our memories of talking in British accents about fiddling mittens on eight-mile runs!

Dave and Michelle Borowsky – Thank you for teaching me the importance of leadership at such a young age. You taught me how to own my own faith in God. I am so thankful for your guidance and words of affirmation over the years.

All those who endorsed this book with your kind words – Thank you for having faith in my writing and me! Your positive words have meant more to me than you will ever know.

Fine Arts Leaders – I would not be who I am today without the blessing of Fine Arts. It helped me discover so many things that I love to do, like acting and songwriting. Thanks for everything you have done for all the kids involved in this amazing opportunity. You have equipped this generation of young people to stand up for the word of God.

Mrs. Beatty – You inspire me in so many ways! When I'm a teacher, I want to be just like you! A lot of my favorite memories of high school were in your class. Thank you for making my love of drama and theater grow.

Every other teacher, coach, administrator, and staff member at Clare Public Schools – Thank you for all the support you have shown me. I am beyond grateful to have ended up in Clare.

Everyone at Spring Arbor University, including Coach Burk and Chaplain Ron Kopicko – Thank you for caring about my family and me. I'm proud to call myself a Cougar!

Clare Assembly of God Family – Thank you for being my support system. Thank you for providing a second home for me these past several years.

My Grandparents – Richard Donovan, Donna Cummings, Thomas Nutt, and Kathy Nutt—I love you all so dearly. Thanks for the prayers, texts, and calls. It's a blessing to be related to you!

My aunts, uncles, and crazy cousins – There are very few things that make me happier than being together with all of you. I truly appreciate all of the encouragement you have given me toward my running career and other aspects of my life.

The Single Cousins Club (Victoria, Matthew, and Anna) – You guys make me laugh like no one else does, and your silly Snapchats always make my day. I love our long Jesus talks!

My friends – You know who you are! Thank you for the moments of singing late at night or watching sappy chick flicks. Thank you for being the best teammates. Thank you for reaffirming my love of anything chocolate. Thank you for laughing loudly in class with me. Thank you for the funny smirks in the school hallways. Thank you for the countless selfie photo shoots. Thank you for entertaining me with your sass. Thank you for praying with me and worshipping with me. Thank you for believing in me with this book. I love you!

My sister Autumn, and her husband, Tim – My heart is so full whenever I'm with you! Autumn, I strive to be as caring as you are. You have so much passion for other people. Tim, you are an amazing listener and also an amazing storyteller. You're one of the funniest guys I know! The love of God flows out of you both.

My brother Jonathan, and sister-in-law, Addy – Jonathan, thank you for being the "guy version of me," as Addy has described! You have always encouraged me to be bold in the gifts

God has given me. Addy, I am so thankful beyond thankful that you are a part of our family! You are so selfless and humble. Thanks for watching "Dancing With the Stars" with me!

My sister Victoria – Thanks for paving the way for me in so many areas of my life. No one else knows me like you do. I love singing with you and running with you! Your heart for worship inspires me daily. You are so determined in everything you do. God knew what he was doing when he made us sistas!

My parents, Lisa and Scott Harper – Thanks for giving birth to me! I really enjoyed our time together my last few years of high school. I appreciate the close relationships I have with both of you. I cannot thank you enough for embedding a heart of worship in our family. Also, thanks for the running genes! I'm proud to call you my parents!

Love,

Jasmine

ABOUT THE AUTHOR

Jasmine (Jazzy) Harper, a graduate of Clare High School in Clare, MI, is blessed with a love for God and people. Those who know her best would say she is caring and passionate about growing in God. Jasmine has an engaging sense of humor that draws people in and makes anyone feel special.

Jasmine's accolades include earning All-State high school track and cross-country honors at least ten times. In fact, Jasmine holds her high school track records for the 1600 Meters (4:59) and 3200 Meters (11:01). She is the humble recipient of two highly respected awards: the Michigan High School Athletic

Scholar Athlete Award and the Michigan Interscholastic Athletic Administrators Association Scholar Athlete Award.

According to Coach Kyle McKown, *Jasmine is one of the most well-rounded and impressive student athletes I have ever worked with. She embodies strong character traits of loyalty, honestly, modesty, a strong work ethic, and her genuine compassion always brings out the best in the people around her.*

Her leadership and positive influence on others can be seen in the classroom, among her teammates, in the community, in her church, and the various volunteer organizations she works hard to positively impact. Jasmine sees the greater purpose behind her life. Her goal is to glorify God and to focus on the greater lessons of life. The role that God plays in her life positively impacts her interactions with other people, her drive to be the best that she can be, and gives her a greater purpose in which to view the world. Though Jasmine has enjoyed large amounts of success, her modesty always overshadows her accomplishments.

Along with athletics, Jasmine thoroughly enjoys discovering, developing, and deploying Fine Arts gifts for the glory of God. She has competed in over twenty categories within Michigan Fine Arts Festivals since the age of seven, and participated at the National Fine Arts Festivals with the Assemblies of God since she was twelve. Jasmine earned the Superior with Honors ratings in the areas of Small Human Video, Large Drama, Small Vocal Ensemble, Unconventional Percussion, Spoken Word, Short Sermon, Songwriting, Rap Solo, and Digital Photography. In addition, Jasmine won Merit Awards (first in the state) for Drama Solo, Songwriting Modern Hymn, Drama Ensemble Small, Small Human Video, Human Video Solo, Readers Theater, Small Vocal Ensemble, and Children's Lesson Solo. National distinctions include eighth in the nation in Small Drama Ensemble, fourth in the nation in Readers Theater, and fourth in the nation in her Songwriting Modern Hymn. With all of this Jasmine declares, "To God be the glory."

Jasmine is thrilled to study elementary education while running track and cross-country at the highly acclaimed Spring Arbor University, her first and only college choice.

Among Jasmine's favorite activities are leading worship at her home church of Clare Assembly of God, singing tight harmonies with her siblings, enjoying time with friends, eating mint chocolate chip ice cream, and hanging out with family on the pristine beaches of Lake Michigan.

To contact Jasmine for speaking opportunities, musical events, and dramatic engagements, visit extendeddevo.com, email jasmine@extendeddevo.com, or call 734-775-3073.

If you are encouraged by *Extended*, you can further connect with Jasmine by visiting:

Instagram: @jasmineharperblog
Facebook: @jasmineharperauthor
Website: extendeddevo.com
Email: jasmine@extendeddevo.com

Made in the USA
Lexington, KY
20 October 2017